Klamkin, Marian.
White House china

NK
3730
.W37
W484
Copy 1

12.50

DATE			

WOODSON REGIONAL CENTER
9525 SOUTH HALSTED ST.

White House China

PLATE 1 *Top* This is a Lincoln reproduction made during time of the centennial celebration in 1876. The Washington States plate and the Grant, Hayes, and Lincoln plates have all been reproduced by Haviland. (*Private collection. Photograph by Charles Klamkin.*)

Bottom Plate from Monroe dessert service. Vignettes in border represent commerce, agriculture, art, science, and strength. Made by Dagoty of Paris. (*Private collection. Photograph by Charles Klamkin.*)

PLATE 2 *Right* Urn from Monroe state dessert service. Hand-painted and gilded. (*Private collection. Photograph by Charles Klamkin.*)

White House China

MARIAN KLAMKIN

Charles Scribner's Sons New York

Copyright © 1972 Marian Klamkin

This book published simultaneously in the
United States of America and in Canada—
Copyright under the Berne Convention

All rights reserved. No part of this book may be reproduced in any form
without the permission of Charles Scribner's Sons.

A—8.72 [Mz]

Printed in the United States of America
Library of Congress Catalog Card Number 72–179553
SBN 684–12758–X (trade cloth)

To Charles

PLATE 3 *Above* Reverse of Hayes fish plate (see Plate 20), showing gilded lobster claws as feet for plate. (*Collection of Marjorie W. Hardy. Photograph by Charles Klamkin.*)

Above Bowl from Washington's Cincinnati service purchased in 1786. (*The Smithsonian Institution*)

Left Side of the Jackson punch bowl has eagle in flight against sunburst. (*Collection of Marjorie W. Hardy. Photograph by Charles Klamkin.*)

PLATE 4

Top left Printed earthenware plate, Staffordshire, owned by Zachary Taylor and used in White House. (*Private collection. Photograph by Charles Klamkin.*)

Top right Service plate from Lyndon Johnson state china, showing adoption of Monroe eagle in center and floral border. (*The Smithsonian Institution.*)

Bottom left Breakfast plate from Harrison state china shows reverse of colors in border. (*Collection of Marjorie W. Hardy. Photograph by Charles Klamkin.*)

Bottom right Gold-bordered Eisenhower service plate, made by Castleton, to be used with the Truman state china. (*The Smithsonian Institution*)

Acknowledgments

I would like to express my gratitude to three people who, more than any others, were responsible for giving me the help necessary to complete this book. First, I would like to thank my husband, Charles, without whose photographic talent and general help the work could never have been accomplished. I am most grateful for the generous aid given to me by two collectors of Presidential china, Mrs. Marjorie Hardy and a gentleman who prefers to remain anonymous. Permission to study both collections and to photograph them was essential to the completion of this work. Moreover, the sharing of knowledge and source material was extremely helpful and is sincerely appreciated.

I would like to thank the following people for their efforts in helping me gather information for this book: Mr. James R. Ketchum, former Curator of the White House, Mr. Clement E. Conger, present Curator of the White House and his staff; Dr. Keith Melder, Miss Barbara Coffee, and especially Mr. Herbert R. Collins of the Department of Political History and Technology, Smithsonian Institution.

I am grateful for the help I received from Mr. Clarence W. Lyons of the National Archives, Washington, D.C.; Mr. Charles Blitzer, Assistant Secretary for History and Art, Smithsonian Institution; Mr. Watt P. Marchman, Director, The Rutherford B. Hayes Library; Mr. Stanley W. McClure, Chief, National Memorials Branch, Lincoln Museum; Mr. James E. O'Neill, Director, Hyde Park, and his curatorial and library staffs; Mrs. Lois L. Childers, Curator, President Benjamin Harrison Homes; Mr. Douglas B. Green, Research Assistant, The Hermitage; Miss Christine Meadows, Curator, The Mount Vernon Ladies Association; and Mrs. Joyce Reid and her staff at the Watertown (Connecticut) Library.

I would also like to thank Miss Helene Lindow, personal secretary to Mrs. Lyndon B. Johnson and Mrs. Lyndon B. Johnson for her office's prompt reply and release of necessary information on the Johnson china. A special thanks is offered to Mrs. Dwight D. Eisenhower for sending necessary and interesting information.

Others who were helpful in various ways during the period of research required by the subject matter are: Mr. Eric Hatch, Chairman, State of Connecticut Historical Commission; Senator Lowell P. Weiker, Jr.; Mr. Barry W. Sullivan, Manager, Promotion Coordination, Lenox, Inc.; Mr. Frederick Haviland, Vice President, Haviland and Company; and Mr. Derek Halfpenny, Public Relations Officer, Josiah Wedgwood and Sons, Ltd.; and the curatorial staff of the Wedgwood Museum, Barlaston, Stoke-on-Trent, England.

I am especially grateful to Mr. James Oliver Brown and Miss Elinor Parker for their effort in behalf of this book.

Contents

Acknowledgments viii
List of Illustrations xi
1. The White House China Room   3
2. George Washington   1789–1797   12
3. John Adams   1797–1801   21
4. Thomas Jefferson   1801–1809   24
5. James Madison   1809–1817   27
6. James Monroe   1817–1825   31
7. John Quincy Adams   1825–1829   38
8. Andrew Jackson   1829–1837   40
9. Martin Van Buren   1837–1841   43
10. William Henry Harrison   1841   46
11. John Tyler   1841–1845   48
12. James Knox Polk   1845–1849   50
13. Zachary Taylor   1849–1850   52
14. Millard Fillmore   1850–1853   54
15. Franklin Pierce   1853–1857   56
16. James Buchanan   1857–1861   59

17. *Abraham Lincoln   1861–1865   70*
18. *Andrew Johnson   1865–1869   74*
19. *Ulysses Simpson Grant   1869–1877   76*
20. *Rutherford Birchard Hayes   1877–1881   82*
21. *James Abram Garfield   1881   90*
22. *Chester Alan Arthur   1881–1885   92*
23. *Grover Cleveland   1885–1889, 1893–1897   95*
24. *Benjamin Harrison   1889–1893   98*
25. *William McKinley   1897–1901   102*
26. *Theodore Roosevelt   1901–1909   104*
27. *William Howard Taft   1909–1913   109*
28. *Woodrow Wilson   1913–1921   113*
29. *Warren Gamaliel Harding   1921–1923   120*
30. *Calvin Coolidge   1923–1929   122*
31. *Herbert Clark Hoover   1929–1933   124*
32. *Franklin Delano Roosevelt   1933–1945   127*
33. *Harry S Truman   1945–1953   131*
34. *Dwight David Eisenhower   1953–1961   133*
35. *John Fitzgerald Kennedy   1961–1963   137*
36. *Lyndon Baines Johnson   1963–1969   139*
37. *Richard Milhous Nixon   1969 —   143*
38. *Reproductions of Presidential China   144*
39. *Auctions of Private Collections of Presidential China   150*
    Author's Note   161
    Bibliography   165
    Index   171

Color Illustrations

Plate 1   Lincoln reproduction made in 1876
                Monroe dessert plate

Plate 2   Urn from Monroe dessert service

Plate 3   Reverse of Hayes fish plate
                Bowl from Washington's Cincinnati service
                Jackson punch bowl

Plate 4   Plate owned by Zachary Taylor
                Lyndon Johnson service plate
                Harrison breakfast plate
                Eisenhower service plate

Plate 5   Teapot underdish from Mount Vernon
                Martha Washington sugar bowl
                Blue Willow pattern plate (Washington)

Plate 6   Plate from Washington Cincinnati service
                Niderviller bowl (Washington)
                Washington dinner plate
                Sèvres tureen (Adams)

Plate 7   Sèvres serving plate (Adams)
Sèvres dinner service plate (Adams)
French porcelain teapot (Madison)

Plate 8   Plate from Madison tea service
Dolley Madison cup and saucer
Madison serving plate
Dinner service plate (Madison)

Plate 9   French porcelain plate (Madison)
Compote from Monroe service
Footed bowl from Monroe service
Faïence plate (Monroe)

Plate 10 German porcelain plate (John Quincy Adams)
John Quincy Adams tureen
John Quincy Adams plate

Plate 11 John Quincy Adams Meissen china
Bloor-Derby serving plate (John Quincy Adams)
Jackson compote

Plate 12 Jackson soup bowl
Jackson dinner plate
Spode cup and saucer (Van Buren)
Log-cabin pitcher (W. H. Harrison)
Punch bowl of French porcelain (Jackson)

Plate 13 French porcelain dessert plate (Polk)
Bisque kneeling figures on fruit basket (Tyler)
Polk dessert plate

Plate 14 Franklin Pierce china
French porcelain dessert plate (Polk)
Polk dinner plate
Franklin Pierce plate

Plate 15 Haviland plate (probably Buchanan)
Haviland centerpiece (probably Buchanan)
Footed compote by Haviland
Chipped Buchanan plate
Interior of compote

Plate 16 French porcelain cup (Lincoln)
Abraham Lincoln plate, compote and small platter
Buff-bordered plate and gravy boat (Lincoln)

Plate 17   Lincoln serving plate
Andrew Johnson earthenware plate
Rose-bordered plate (Grant)
Royal Worcester plate (Lincoln)

Plate 18   Dinner plate from Grant service
Grant dinner plate
Oyster plate from Hayes service
Reverse of oyster plate
Hayes soup bowl

Plate 19   Soup plate with Indian (Hayes)
Plate with Indian design (Hayes)
Soup plate from Hayes service
Reverse of the soup plate
"Pecan" dessert plate (Hayes)
Hayes game plate

Plate 20   "California Quail" plate (Hayes)
Turkey platter (Hayes)
"Fish Series" plate (Hayes)
"Woodcock" game plate (Hayes)

Plate 21   Garfield plate
Chester Arthur plate
Floral Arthur plate
Royal Worcester soup plate (Arthur)

Plate 22   Rose-bordered plate (Arthur)
Grover Cleveland saucer
Wedgwood plate with roses (Cleveland)
Harrison Limoges plates

Plate 23   Breakfront display of Harrison china
Harrison state dinner plate
Haviland cup and saucer (McKinley or Cleveland)

Plate 24   Theodore Roosevelt china
Roosevelt menu cover
Roosevelt plate

Plate 25   Taft Breakfast service
Minton cup and saucer (Taft)
Wilson service plate
"Liberty" tea service (Wilson)

Plate 26   F.D.R. official state china
Lenox service china (Truman)
Eisenhower birthday plate

Plate 27   Madison china displayed in the White House
President's dining room, showing Lincoln china
L.B.J. dinner and salad plates

Plate 28   Bowls from Johnson china
Washington States plate reproduction
Washington States plate reproduced in 1932

Black-and-white Illustrations

Fig. 1 White House china collection in Theodore Roosevelt's administration
Fig. 2 Drawing of Washington decanter
Fig. 3 Sugar bowl from Martha Washington's States china
Fig. 4 Underside of Niderviller bowl (Washington)
Fig. 5 Sèvres plate and Angoulême bowl (Washington)
Fig. 6 Reverse of above plates
Fig. 7 Drawing of Jefferson china
Fig. 8 Serving dish and plates (Madison)
Fig. 9 Monroe state dinner pattern
Fig. 10 Plate used during Monroe administration
Fig. 11 Drawing of Polk fruit basket, cup and saucer
Fig. 12 Drawing of Pierce dinner plates
Fig. 13 Engraving of two plates designed for Franklin Pierce
Fig. 14 Plate and custard cup attributed to James Buchanan
Fig. 15 Drawing of Lincoln punch bowl
Fig. 16 Double-handled custard cup from Lincoln state china
Fig. 17 Dinner invitation sent by President and Mrs. Grant
Fig. 18 Mark used on some Grant china
Fig. 19 Dinner plate from Grant administration
Fig. 20 Mark on Grant soup bowl
Fig. 21 Obverse and reverse of Hayes plate

xv

Fig. 22   Drawing of White House china collection in 1908
Fig. 23   China selected by Mrs. Grover Cleveland
Fig. 24   Drawing of Benjamin Harrison plates and goblet
Fig. 25   Mark on reverse of Benjamin Harrison china
Fig. 26   White House china selected by Mrs. Theodore Roosevelt
Fig. 27   Dinner plate from Wilson service
Fig. 28   Lenox service plate, bouillon cup and saucer from Wilson service
Fig. 29   Blue-bordered plate (Harding)
Fig. 30   Plate representing Coolidge administration
Fig. 31   Wedgwood plate owned by Herbert Hoover
Fig. 32   Plate donated by Herbert Hoover
Fig. 33   Mark on reverse of F. D. Roosevelt china
Fig. 34   Legend on reverse of Eisenhower birthday plate
Fig. 35   Markings on reverse of Shenango Washington plate
Fig. 36   Mark on centennial reproduction of Lincoln plate
Fig. 37   Mark on reverse of Grant centennial reproduction
Fig. 38   Auction catalogue of Presidential china
Fig. 39   Washington Cincinnati plate

White House China

CHAPTER 1

The White House China Room

On the ground floor of the White House, next to the Diplomatic Reception Room and directly under the East Room, is a room that houses the White House Presidential china collection. This collection represents pottery and porcelain used in the Executive Mansion by each successive Presidential family, beginning with George Washington. Unfurnished except for a carpet, the China Room has cabinets with glass doors built into three of its walls and is used for no other purpose but to house the collection of china, silver, and glass. On the window sill of the fourth wall is a tall white china bowl on a pedestal that has blue and gold decoration. This is the most elaborate china object in the room, and it is protected by a glass case. On the opposite side of the same wall hangs a large portrait of Grace Coolidge and her dog.

The history of the china collection in the White House does not date as far back as one might think. Until recently it had always been the privilege of each incoming administration to clean out any unwanted objects from the White House, and parts of dinner, tea, and dessert services were seldom kept. Interest in gathering relics of Presidential china began during the administration of William McKinley, and the existence of the present collection of china is due more to the work of a Washington writer than to any First Lady who occupied the White House.

Research on the subject of Presidential china by Abby Gunn Baker, who subsequently wrote many articles on the subject, came about in a strange manner. General Theodore A. Bingham, superintendent of public buildings and grounds in Washington in 1901, who was responsible for the supervision of the White House, had worked at European embassies in his earlier days. He told Mrs. Baker that he thought it a shame that no care or veneration was bestowed on the belongings of the President's mansion. As a result of General Bingham's interest, Mrs. McKinley invited Mrs. Baker to spend the summer at the White House studying the china and plate. The eventual result of this invitation was the gathering of the first collection of Presidential china in the White House. At that time not a single complete china service remained at the President's house.

Two First Ladies, previous to this time, had made some effort to gather a collection of china representing past administrations, but neither effort had materialized into a White House collection. Mrs. Rutherford B. Hayes planned a collection, but since she was not able to complete it in time to present it to the government before her husband's term expired, she simply moved the collection to Fremont, Ohio, when the family returned there. Mrs. Hayes probably correctly assumed that if she left the collection, nothing further would be done with it in any case.

The next First Lady to show an interest in the china of the former administrations was Mrs. Benjamin Harrison, who had taught ceramic painting to young ladies before her marriage. Of her, Mrs. Baker wrote, "Mrs. Harrison probably did more to awaken a sentiment to save the historic furnishings of the White House than any of her predecessors. One of her cherished ambitions was to make a collection of the Presidential ware, and which she hoped to have built into the walls of the state dining room, where the ware could be preserved and displayed." Mrs. Harrison was not able to accomplish this, and nothing further was done to preserve examples of White House china until after the turn of the century.

The earliest published indication that anyone thought it odd that no regard for the historical importance of pottery and porcelain representing the various administrations was apparent is found in the book *China Collecting in America*, by Alice Morse Earle, published in 1892. Mrs. Earle, who discussed some of the china used by Presidents, said, "It seems a pity that a few pieces of each of these 'state sets' should not have been preserved in a cabinet at the White House to show us the kind of china from which our early rulers ate their daily meals and served their state dinners, as well as to show us our varying and halting progress in luxury, refinement and taste."

By the time Abby Gunn Baker made her study in 1901, not more than seven administrations were represented by china left in the White House. These plates were from the Lincoln, Grant, Hayes, Arthur, Cleveland, Harrison, and McKinley administrations. Mrs. Baker said that of these, she found evidence that only Lincoln, Hayes, and Grant had ordered complete dinner services. It was not unusual in the nineteenth century for plates to be purchased by the dozen as needed, and a study of vouchers in the National Archives indicates that this was often done in order to provide enough plates to serve whatever was the number of guests attending state dinners in the White House at a particular time.

Circumstances were not to allow Mrs. McKinley to receive full credit for her interest in gathering a White House china collection, and by the time that Mrs. Baker's proposed article was completed, in December of 1901, President McKinley had been assassinated and Mrs. Theodore Roosevelt was First Lady. General Bingham was succeeded by Colonel Thomas W. Symons as superintendent of public buildings and grounds, and he became interested in the project after reading Mrs. Baker's article. Colonel Symons evidently had little difficulty in convincing Mrs. Roosevelt that work on the china collection should be continued. Mrs. Roosevelt had two cabinets built in the lower corridor of the White House and invited Mrs. Baker to select the pieces of china that should be placed in them.

President Roosevelt approved of the work that Mrs. Baker had done and suggested that all Presidents be represented in the collection, whereupon Mrs. Baker began her search for more china. She used the medium of the press to plead for gifts or loans to the collection by descendants of former Presidents. Mrs. Baker wrote that Mrs. Roosevelt refused to purchase any of the china, since she "desired that the collection should be a patriotic one, and the pieces for it should either be given or loaned rather than purchased." Mrs. Baker reported that many pieces were forthcoming for the collection, but certainly not as many as might have been taken from private hands if the government had been willing to purchase the china from private collectors. However, it is obvious that Mrs. Baker and Mrs. Roosevelt were both dedicated to the task of finding pieces of china that could be authenticated. Since many of the Presidents had purchased china that was offered on the open market and not especially decorated or monogrammed to order, this became a difficult task, and the problem of authenticity remains to this day. (See Fig. 1.)

This project put more emphasis on the preservation of all historic White House relics and gave Mrs. Roosevelt more insight concerning the previously lax White House disposal policy. She made certain that none of the Roosevelt china would be allowed to get into private hands upon the termination of her husband's administration.

Sad to say, Mrs. Roosevelt had few successors who showed any interest in the china collection. However, she did arrange that the collection be placed under the supervision of the Bureau of Public Buildings and Grounds so that future administrations could not dispose of it. It was not until Mrs. John F. Kennedy lived in the White House that definite rules were established so that no object could be taken from the White House that might have artistic or historical value.

Mrs. Baker continued through many years to write articles to bring attention to the White House china collection, and she became the one recognized expert on the subject of Presidential plates. The sad truth is that Mrs. Baker brought little expertise in the area of ceramics history to the White House collection and that a great many errors in attribution were made. This is particularly true of china purchased previous to the Lincoln administration. The word of amateur historians became accepted as fact, and some donors, anxious to be immortalized in the President's mansion, hastened to add more legend and fiction concerning their donations. Private collectors also hastened to add more Presidential plates to their collections, fully realizing that Mrs. Baker's publicity was increasing the value of what they owned.

There is, today, a great deal of confusion concerning the china of our early Presidents. Mrs. Baker was not well versed in the history of ceramics, nor was she familiar with the decorative art styles of the various periods of the nineteenth century. She did not possess sufficient knowledge to describe specimens of china in terms of national origins. At the beginning of this century, so little had been written on the subject of pottery and porcelain that Abby Gunn Baker is to be forgiven for much of the misinformation surrounding the White House china collection.

At the time of the Wilson administration the collection had, according to Mrs. Baker, outgrown the two black walnut cabinets that Mrs. Roosevelt had placed in the lower corridor of the mansion, and Mrs. Wilson set aside "the large and sunny room at the foot of the stairway on the main corridor" and designated it for the china representing the Presidents.

When President Wilson's china service was delivered, Mrs. Baker was asked to write a press release describing the White House china collection. This same release seems to have been added to by later administrations, and it was used again to describe the collection and the Franklin Roosevelt, Harry Truman, and Dwight Eisenhower china when each service was purchased. Evidently no effort had been made in those intervening years to study and catalogue the collection. Press secretaries obviously simply pulled Mrs. Baker's history out of the White House files, added something about the latest china purchased, and handed the same old information to the press.

Fig. 1 The White House china collection during Theodore Roosevelt's administration, when it was organized by Abby Gunn Baker. (*The Smithsonian Institution*)

The China Room gained some attention during the Truman administration when the White House was completely renovated. New cabinets were built to house the collection, and the room was paneled with pine boards removed from other parts of the building. Proper lighting was installed inside the cabinets. The pine paneling has since been painted white.

It was not until the Eisenhower administration that new interest was awakened in the china collection. Mrs. Eisenhower arranged for the addition of china representing five administrations not previously owned, and some reclassifications were made. In June, 1958, a new press release describing the White House china collection was written. It contains a great many equivocations in attributions such as "believed to be," "said to be," "reputedly," and "probably." Many of the descriptions are extremely vague. For example:

> William McKinley—1897–1901
> Several family pieces, including both Mintons and Wedgewood [sic].

> Chester A. Arthur—1881–1885
> A half dozen assorted dessert plates, two of which are particularly interesting in their generous use of gold or silver.

It is obvious that as late as 1958, no one who might have brought to it any knowledge of ceramics had catalogued the collection. This same release, written with the aid of Smithsonian political historians, suggests that the famous Hayes china "was purchased abroad and decorated here in the United States." Slight research would have informed the compiler of this list that the Hayes china was decorated in France, although an American artist, Theodore Davis, painted the original designs for the plates.

Despite the several curators of the White House who have come and gone since the Kennedy administration, it appears that no effort has been made to catalogue the china collection with regard to proving some of the attributions. Only photographs of a few plates that have already appeared in White House publications are available for study, so that no outside source can properly study the collection. There seem to be no photographs of the reverse sides of the plates available at the White House for study, and thus no maker's marks or decorator's signatures can be proved. Although some similar plates are part of the Smithsonian collection of Presidential china, a large portion of the White House collection is unique in the country, and it is unfortunate that the china is treated more as a curiosity than as a true museum collection.

Interestingly, the China Room is not open to the general public during the morning tour of the White House. This privilege is reserved only for a favored group, usually relatives and important constituents of senators and congressmen, who are brought through the public rooms of the White House before it is opened to the general public. Since the china collection is the only continuous collection in the White House, representing all the administrations, it is difficult to believe that it might not be of interest to many of the regular tourists. However, the room is small, and the logistics of bringing thousands of people through might be next to impossible.

Although there is still much work to be done in the study of Presidential china, it is obvious that the country owes a debt to the few First Ladies who realized the importance of salvaging the remaining examples before they became so many broken dishes. In our time, Mrs. Eisenhower, Mrs. Kennedy, and Mrs. Johnson all had a strong sense of history of the house they occupied and the objects with which it was furnished.

In the attempt to gather specific information on the subject of Presidential china, it was obvious from the start that early writers on the subject were not to be completely trusted. A great deal of the published information is contradictory. For some reason, the legends and myths surrounding the White House pottery and porcelain have been allowed to grow until it is almost impossible to untangle many of the early attributions of certain plates. Nor is it possible to consult government records that might have shed some light on the subject. Although the White House is said to have records of purchase that go back as far as 1817, these records are unavailable for study. The author's request to study these records was denied by the present White House curator, Clement E. Conger, who said, "We regret that our records are not available to persons outside the White House for security reasons."

There is a collection of Presidential china on display at the Smithsonian Institution in Washington. It is at the Smithsonian that one would expect to untangle some of the mysteries surrounding the dinner, tea, and dessert services used during the various administrations of Presidents and their families. Since Mrs. Eisenhower placed the White House collection in the custodianship of the Smithsonian, it was to be hoped that information on the collection would also be available for study at the national museum. Such does not seem to be the case. The files offered at the Smithsonian for study on the subject contained little more than copies of early magazine articles and some photographs of the Smithsonian collection. Examples of Presidential china that are on display are spread throughout the various period-room displays and are as nebulously labeled as the White House china. A concerted effort to find out if more definite information was available at the Smithsonian Institution led nowhere.

This lack of specific information leads one to believe that much of the attribution in the area of Presidential china is based on legend, wishful thinking, and conjecture. Only where a proper study has been done, such as at Mount Vernon, can one take as fact the claims made in attribution of many of the china pieces. The majority of nineteenth-century Presidential pottery and porcelain is still a matter of legend, since little attention has been paid to the eventual historical value of White House furnishings until fairly recently. President Monroe was aware of some of the problems that would exist with each new tenant of the White House concerning the preservation and care of the furnishings. But Congress gave the issue little or no attention except to criticize the purchases of some of the unpopular Presidents.

Even the early articles written on the subject of Presidential china must be approached with a certain amount of skepticism, since most of the attributions can be traced to Mrs. Baker. Attributions are currently being made by historians who can find little proof in National Archives vouchers that might list, typically, "6 doz. plates" or "3 doz. cups." Identification cards in the White House and Smithsonian collections are rampant with equivocal "said-to-bes," "attributed-tos," and "probablys." In many cases no further proof can ever be found to link certain plates with the families that truly owned them.

As the United States approaches its two hundredth year, one would hope that our museums and the people who run them would apply the knowledge of antiquarians and historians in sorting out the objects that reflect our heritage. Although this is being done in some areas of "made in America" items, a certain amount of embarrassment seems to exist in the area of fine porcelain and pottery, which we had to purchase from other nations until this century. A knowledge of the development of ceramic art in America would inform anyone that our First Families had little choice, until the beginning of this century, but to send to France, Germany, China, and England for the plates from which they ate.

Although sources at government institutions speak of the private collections of Presidential china as though the ownership were in doubt, or should be, it has historically been the private collectors of Presidential china who have made attempts to attribute properly those relics that they own through the neglect of many of the Presidents and their wives to foresee the historic value of the objects and who sent the plates to secondhand dealers and put them in auctions.

Many of the plates and other objects illustrated here have never before been displayed publicly or appeared in photographs in any publication. It is to be hoped that this book will bring to light more information and other collections, so that eventually the entire story of Presidential china will be pieced together. *White House China* can be considered only a beginning, an attempt to untangle some of the myths concerning the plates used in the White House by our Presidents. Some discussion of the ladies who served as official hostesses in the White House throughout its history has been included, since it is felt that the china should not be considered as impersonal objects, but rather as an integral part of the entertaining that has been done by our heads of state and a reflection of their tastes.

It is to be hoped that the publication of this volume will aid in dispelling many of the legends concerning the subject of Presidential china. It would also be desirable that the "porcelain curtain" which surrounds the china collections at the White House and the Smithsonian Institution be lifted so that more of our citizens will be able to see the China Room and so that the collection in our national museum will be made available for proper study and cataloguing. Until that happens, it is doubtful that many of the unique and heretofore unseen, privately owned objects that are illustrated here will find their way to a permanent place in our national collections.

CHAPTER 2

George Washington
1789–1797

Shortly after George Washington's marriage to the young widow Martha Dandridge Custis, in 1759, Washington ordered tableware in an assortment that typifies the ceramics then used by wealthy American households. Mugs, sweetmeat plates, milk pans, custard cups, pickle plates, cups and saucers, and dinner plates were ordered. This type of purchase was not new to Washington, however, who even before his marriage had equipped Mount Vernon with table china and punch bowls. The earliest records indicate that before the Revolution, the Washington ceramics were made in England. An assortment of pewter plates was also ordered before the war.

"Cream coloured ware" chamber pots were mentioned in the early Washington orders, and these were probably Josiah Wedgwood's Queen's ware, a cream-colored earthenware that was light in body and lead glazed. Washbasins with bottles in blue and white were also sent from Staffordshire.

In the custom of the time, the master of Mount Vernon was in charge of all household purchases, and the orders for china were a matter of his choice and taste. One of the earliest purchases after Washington's marriage was for a child's tea set for Martha Washington's daughter by her first marriage.

Fig. 2 Drawing, made in 1908, of the Washington decanter and other pieces, including Canton plate. At that time, these were the only Washington pieces in the White House. *(From The Century Magazine, October, 1908. Drawing by Harry Fenn. Photograph by Charles Klamkin.)*

Richard Farrar and Company of London sent Washington a "Complete sett of Table China fine blue and white" in 1763, but it is not known whether this set, numbering 57 pieces, was English-made or of Chinese origin. Certainly a supply of export porcelain of the Canton type was used at Mount Vernon and elsewhere in the colonies in the latter half of the eighteenth century. However, by this time Staffordshire potters were making their own version of blue and white pottery in the Willow pattern in order to compete with the Chinese product. The discovery of transfer printing in England made it possible for the British potters to produce reasonably priced blue and white plates that were destined to become the popular tableware for most Americans during the first half of the nineteenth century. There is evidence that large quantities of this ware were purchased by Washington for the Presidential household in Philadelphia. (See Plate 5.)

The Revolutionary War dealt a terrible blow to Staffordshire potters, who had depended upon business from the American colonies to sustain them. French china became fashionable following the war, particularly among the wealthy. When Washington, as our first President, moved to the house previously owned by Comte de Moustier, the French minister to the United States, a large amount of the Count's furnishings and porcelain was purchased for the President's use in the New York mansion. It was shortly before this that Washington commissioned Gouverneur Morris, who was in Paris at the time, to purchase table ornaments; and it is probable that table china was sent to Washington at the same time.

During George Washington's term of office and later, when the Washingtons returned to Mount Vernon, our first President entertained constantly; and Washington continued to order china until he owned a large supply. This accounts for the large amount of Washington china that remains today in contrast with later Presidents, for whom there are few surviving examples of the tableware they used. The custom in the late eighteenth century of presenting guests with mementos of their visits has accounted for many odd pieces of known Mount Vernon china that have been discovered throughout the years.

There are three china patterns that are most closely associated with George and Martha Washington. The first of these is the service known as the "Cincinnati" table service. This service was purchased on Washington's orders by Colonel Henry Lee in New York in 1786. Three hundred and two pieces were purchased, and Washington's records indicate that £45.5.0 was the price paid. China decorated with the emblem of the Society of the Cincinnati had previously been purchased by Major Samuel Shaw, an active member of the society. However, it is believed that the Washington set is the only one in which the Cincinnati emblem is held by a figure of Fame. Martha Washington willed the remainder of this china to her grandson, George Washington Parke Custis, and thirteen pieces of this famous porcelain have been returned to Mount Vernon. The White House, the Smithsonian Institution, and the Metropolitan Museum also have examples of the Cincinnati service. (See Plate 3.)

A tea service known as the "Martha Washington," "Monogram," or "States" china is perhaps the pattern most associated with the Washingtons. Certainly it

Fig. 3   Sugar bowl and cup saucer from Martha Washington's States china. (*The Smithsonian Institution*)

is the pattern that has been most often reproduced. This pattern is monogrammed with "MW" and has a chain border with each link enclosing the name of one of the fifteen states of the Union at the time the service was made. A narrow border, in the motif of a snake with its tail in its mouth, surrounds the outer edge of these plates. The Latin motto, DECUS ET TUTAMEN AB ILLO ("A glory and a defense of it"), is written on a ribbon motif under the center monogram, which is applied over a gold sunburst. The Cantonese service was a gift to Martha Washington from Andrea van Braam Houckgeest, a representative of the Dutch East India Company, who settled in America in 1796. Records indicate that "a Box of China for Lady Washington" was a part of his cargo on his ship, *Lady Louisa*, which sailed into Philadelphia on April 24, 1796. (See Fig. 3.)

Mrs. Washington bequeathed the remainder of this tea service, of which there are thought to have been 45 pieces originally, to her grandson. Evidence also exists that a custard cup and saucer of the set were presented by the Custis family to Lafayette during his historic visit to this country in 1824–1825.

Fig. 4   Underside of Niderviller bowl, showing mark. (*The Smithsonian Institution*)

Although the two services discussed above were made in China, a third set of Washington porcelain is of French origin. This is the Niderviller table service presented to the Washingtons by Comte de Custine, owner of the Niderviller factory. The main decoration on this service is the monogram "GW" painted over a gold-brown cloud. A chaplet of roses is painted above the monogram. A variety of borders decorate the various pieces of this white porcelain. The service was presented to the Washingtons in 1782 by a group of French officers who had fought with the Americans during the Revolution. (See Fig. 4, Plate 6.)

The table service generally accepted as the Washington state service is made up of white French porcelain that is undecorated except for a narrow gilt edging. The original pieces in this service were a part of the household goods purchased from the Comte de Moustier in 1790. These early plates were Sèvres. It is thought that Washington added to this service during the period that he was President and lived in New York and Philadelphia.

White French porcelain with gilded edges was also purchased by Washington. It is simpler in shape than the Sèvres china, but it was obviously compatible with the original service. This china bears the marks of the Angoulême and Nast potteries. (See Figs. 5, 6.)

Chinese export porcelain, in stock patterns, was purchased from time to time by Washington. Punch bowls, mugs, and chocolate cups were also added to the supplies at Mount Vernon.

A blue and gold ornamented service made by the Caughley pottery in England has been documented as part of a Washington dinner or dessert service. Obviously, it is more difficult to attribute pieces of stock china than it is to attribute the services that are monogrammed or otherwise absolutely identifiable as having belonged to the Washingtons. It is only when some sort of record exists with an object that provenance can be accepted as definite. A record such as *A Descriptive Catalogue of a Portion of the Contents of my Colonial Dining Hall at my Home, No. 78 Wethersfield Avenue, Comprising Historical Furniture, Silver, Prints, Portraits and Historical China*, written by James Terry in 1905, lists five pieces of documented Washington china: two platters, a vegetable dish, and a cup and saucer. Were it not for Mr. Terry's careful recording of the provenance of these plates, they would not have found their way back to Mount Vernon, where they are currently on loan from Harvard University. (See Plates 5, 6.)

Fig. 5 A Sèvres plate and Angoulême bowl, both white porcelain with gold rim, considered state china of George and Martha Washington. (*The Smithsonian Institution*)

Fig. 6 Reverse of above plates, showing marks. (*The Smithsonian Institution*)

One other piece of pottery of historical importance is listed by Mr. Terry as a "Large, Oval, Blue Pottery Vessel with handles." Of this item, the catalogue (of which there is only one copy) records, "This quaint pottery vessel, or tub, belonged to Mrs. Lawrence Lewis (Nellie Custis) and was used by her at 'Audley' when paring and stewing apples, and other fruit, and was continued in the same use by Mrs. H. L. Daingerfield Lewis, until a check or crack appeared in the bottom, when, as she states, she realized it was of too great historic interest, to be treated in such menial service." Unfortunately, Mr. Terry's typewritten catalogue does not include photographs of these objects.

CHAPTER 3

John Adams
1797–1801

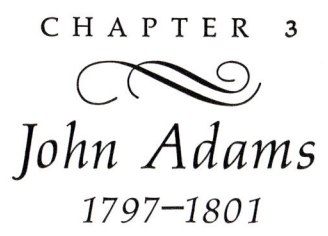

John Adams, second President of the United States, was the first President to occupy the mansion in Washington. He and his wife, Abigail, moved into the building under rather trying conditions. In 1800, Abigail Adams wrote to her daughter about her sentiments concerning her new home:

> The house is upon a grand and superb scale, requiring about thirty servants to attend and keep the apartments in proper order, and perform the ordinary business of the house and stables: an establishment very well proportioned to the President's salary. The lighting the apartments, from the kitchen to parlors and chambers, is a tax indeed; and the fires we are obliged to keep to secure us from daily agues, is another very cheering comfort. To assist us in this great castle, and render less attendance necessary, bells are wholly wanting, not one single one being hung through the whole house, and promises are all you can obtain. This is so great an inconvenience, that I know not what to do, or how to do. The ladies from Georgetown and in the city have many of them visited me. Yesterday I returned fifteen visits,—but such a place as Georgetown appears,—why our Milton is beautiful. But no comparisons;—if they will put me up some bells, and let me have wood enough to keep fires, I design to be pleased. I could content myself almost anywhere three months; but surrounded with forests, can you believe that wood is not to be had, because people cannot be found to cut and cart it?

Mrs. Adams, in the same letter, describes the condition of the Executive Mansion in 1800:

> You must keep all this to yourself, and when asked how I like it, say that I write you the situation is beautiful, which is true. The house is made habitable, but there is not a single apartment finished, and all withinside, except the plastering, has been done since Briesler came. We have not the least fence, yard, or other convenience, without, and the great unfinished audience-room I make a drying room of, to hang up the clothes in. The principal stairs are not up, and will not be this winter. Six chambers are made comfortable; two are occupied by the President and Mr. Shaw; two lower rooms, one for a common parlor and one for a levee room. Up-stairs there is the oval room, which is designed for the drawing-room, and has the crimson furniture in it. It is a very handsome room now, but when completed it will be beautiful. If the twelve years, in which this place has been considered as the future seat of government, had been improved, as they would have been if in New England, very many of the present inconveniences would have been removed. It is a beautiful spot, capable of every improvement, and the more I view it, the more I am delighted with it. Since I sat down to write, I have been called down to a servant from Mount Vernon, with a billet from Major Custis, and a haunch of venison, and a kind, congratulatory letter from Mrs. Lewis, upon my arrival in the city, with Mrs. Washington's love, inviting me to Mount Vernon, where, health permitting, I will go, before I leave this place. . . .
>
> The vessel which has my clothes and other matter is not arrived. The ladies are impatient for a drawing-room; I have no looking-glasses, but dwarfs, for this house; nor a twentieth part lamps enough to light it. Many things were stolen, many were broken, by the removal; amongst the number, my tea-china is more than half missing.

Despite the hardship of living in a new city that was carved from wilderness, President and Mrs. Adams managed to give their first New Year's reception in the mansion in 1801. The house was only partially finished, and little furniture had been purchased. Nevertheless, the reception was held in the upstairs Oval Room with the formality that had been established by the Washingtons in New York and Philadelphia. By spring of that year, Abigail Adams returned to her native Massachusetts in failing health.

During the four months that the Adamses occupied the Presidential mansion, the entertainment was fashioned after European court etiquette, with which John and Abigail Adams were familiar. New England frugality, however, governed the menus. John Adams was to write later, "I held levees once a week, that all my time not be wasted by idle visits. Jefferson's whole eight years was a levee. I dined a large company once or twice a week. Jefferson dined a dozen every day."

Many Adams family relics still exist in The Old House in Quincy, Massachusetts. In the 1930's, a Boston descendant of John Adams sent five pieces of French china to be added to the national collection of Presidential china. The Museum of Fine Arts in Boston owns a Sèvres plate that once belonged to John Adams. It is probable that this china was purchased when Adams was ambassador to France in 1780 and that this was the first china to have been used in the White House. (See Plates 6, 7.)

Unlike the Washington china, which is monogrammed and, therefore, unmistakable as having belonged to the first President, the existing Adams china is difficult to authenticate. A Worcester teapot with cover, displayed at the Art Institute of Chicago in an exhibit that was called "Dinner with the Presidents," held in 1961, is described in the catalogue as "Decorated in enamel colors and gold with cornflower wreaths and scattered blossoms. . . . According to tradition owned by Adams."

CHAPTER 4

Thomas Jefferson
1801–1809

Thomas Jefferson was well known for his good taste and hospitality long before he succeeded John Adams as President of the United States. His most famous meal was served when he was Secretary of State in 1789 in Philadelphia. A dispute had arisen concerning where the national capital should be built, and it had divided the northern and southern members of Congress. Jefferson invited Washington and the leaders of both parties to his home for dinner, where the problem could be discussed. Strongly in favor of the location in Washington on the banks of the Potomac River, Jefferson won his point during that meal.

The master of Monticello was aware of the value of a well-cooked meal as a means of getting state business accomplished. He entertained lavishly at Monticello, and during his years in Washington there were seldom less than four and often as many as fourteen guests at his table. Our first gourmet President collected recipes and hired a French chef. The proximity of Monticello to the White House made it possible for wagonloads of fresh foods to be brought in to supplement White House stores.

At the July 4, 1801, reception held in the Blue Room of the White House by Jefferson, a tradition was started for which subsequent Presidents and First

PLATE 5 *Above* Teapot underdish said to be from Mount Vernon. Chinese export. (*Collection of Marjorie W. Hardy. Photograph by Charles Klamkin.*)

Above Sugar bowl from Martha Washington's Monogram, or States, china service. This pattern is the most frequently reproduced of all Presidential china. (*White House Historical Association. Photograph by National Geographic Society.*)

Left Plate in blue Willow pattern transfer decoration. Gilt rim. Marked "S" for Salopian (Caughley) England. Made about 1780 and part of Washington's china. (*Private collection. Photograph by Charles Klamkin.*)

Below Bowl from Niderviller table service presented to Washington in 1782 by owner of the pottery, the Comte de Custine. A variety of decorative borders was painted on the plates and cups. (*The Smithsonian Institution*)

Above Plate from Washington's Cincinnati service. (*The Smithsonian Institution*)

Above Dinner plate ornamented with gold and blue borders and scattered flowers. Made by Caughley, England, and part of china service belonging to George and Martha Washington. (*Collection of Marjorie W. Hardy. Photograph by Charles Klamkin.*)

Right Sèvres tureen, from a set of china purchased in France by John Adams. (*White House Historical Association. Photograph by National Geographic Society.*)

PLATE 6

PLATE 7

Above Sèvres serving plate with blue cornflowers, used at White House as state china during administration of President John Adams. (*The Smithsonian Institution*)

Left Plate from Sèvres dinner service owned by John Adams. (*The Smithsonian Institution*)

Below Blue, gold, and white French porcelain teapot with butterfly finial on lid. From a service owned by Dolley Madison. (*The Smithsonian Institution*)

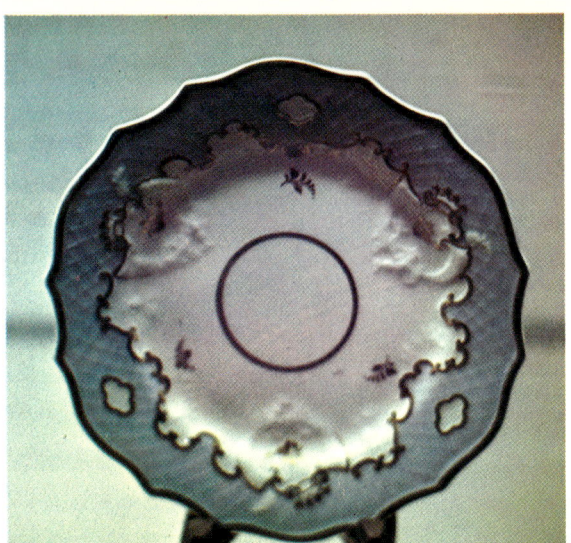

PLATE 8

Left Plate from Dolley Madison tea service. (*The Smithsonian Institution*)

Below Cup and saucer that belonged to Dolley Madison. "Dagoty à Paris." (White House Historical Association. Photograph by National Geographic Society.)

Above Orange-and-black-bordered serving plate made by Nast, a French potter. This pattern is considered to be the state china of the Madison administration. (*The Smithsonian Institution*)

Right Green and white plate and compote cover from a dinner service owned by President Madison. Marked "Dagoty à Paris." (*The Smithsonian Institution*)

PLATE 9

Above Small French porcelain plate with geometrical border in orange and mauve. Said to be from Dolley Madison tea service. (*Collection of Marjorie W. Hardy. Photograph by Charles Klamkin.*)

Right Low compote from Monroe state dessert service. (*Private collection. Photograph by Charles Klamkin.*)

ow Faïence plate with yellow border and painted cus. From Oak Hill, home of President Monroe. (*Collec- of Marjorie W. Hardy. Photograph by Charles Klamkin.*)

Above Footed bowl from Monroe state dessert service. (*Private collection. Photograph by Charles Klamkin.*)

PLATE 10 *Above* Platter from the John Quincy Adams state china. Royal Meissen. (*The Smithsonian Institution*)

Above Tureen from the John Quincy Adams state china. (*The Smithsonian Institution*)

Right German porcelain plate from state china owned by John Quincy Adams. (*The Smithsonian Institution*)

PLATE 11

Top Onion pattern blue and white Meissen china owned by John Quincy Adams. (*The Smithsonian Institution*)

Above Bloor-Derby heart-shaped serving plate with scattered flowers. Said to have been owned by John Quincy Adams. (*Collection of Marjorie W. Hardy. Photograph by Charles Klamkin.*)

Left Blue and gold compote possibly from dessert service owned by President Jackson. (*The Smithsonian Institution*)

Above Soup bowl from Jackson state dinner service. French. (*The Smithsonian Institution*)

Above right Gold-rimmed plate from Jackson dinner service. This pattern was very popular at the time of Jackson's administration. White porcelain. (*Collection of Marjorie W. Hardy. Photograph by Charles Klamkin.*)

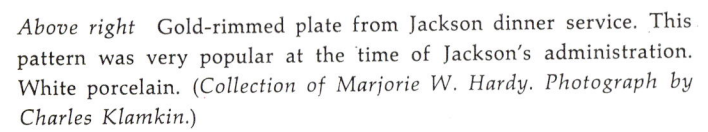

Right Spode gray, gold, and white cup and saucer used at the wedding of Angelica Singleton to Captain Abram Van Buren, son of the President, in 1838. (*The Smithsonian Institution*)

Below right Log-cabin pitcher commemorating William Harrison's political campaign. (*The Smithsonian Institution. Photograph by Charles Klamkin.*)

Below Punch bowl of French porcelain commemorates two weddings held at White House in 1832. A portrait of each bride appears in a center rose on either side of the bowl. This Jackson punch bowl is probably one of the most interesting of all Presidential porcelain relics. (*Collection of Marjorie W. Hardy. Photograph by Charles Klamkin.*)

PLATE 12

Ladies may remember him less than fondly. On this day, the Republican President shook hands with each of his hundred guests. The two previous Presidents had used a formal bow as their greeting.

Thomas Jefferson's lavish entertaining and open hospitality caused him to be literally "eaten out of house and home." Visitors came to Monticello in a steady stream after Jefferson left Washington, and all were wined and dined. This forced Jefferson to build a lodge, Poplar Forest, which had a secret entrance and where he could retreat from visitors. Toward the end of his life, Jefferson

Fig. 7 Drawing, made in 1908, of the Jefferson china presented to the White House by his descendants. The pattern is blue and gold on white, and the porcelain is Chinese export. This china was probably not used in the White House. *(From The Century Magazine, October, 1908. Drawing by Harry Fenn. Photograph by Charles Klamkin.)*

suffered severe financial losses, and following his death, his household effects were sold at auction.

The fact that the Jefferson artifacts were scattered so soon after his death is the reason that so little of the Jefferson china that might still exist can be properly authenticated. It is obvious that he must have owned a large supply of plates. One dinner service does exist about which a legend has grown. This service is Chinese export and is said to have been ordered as state china while Jefferson occupied the White House. However, the china was not delivered; the ship on which it was sent was supposedly captured by pirates before it reached its destination.

The earliest record of the existence of the Jefferson export china can be found in the catalogue of the Governor Lyon auction held on Monday, April 24, 1876. Item 850 describes "A splendid plate of Chinese manufacture with rim and inner border diapered in dark blue relieved by gold tracery. In the centre the letter 'J' in gold is enclosed in a shield, the outline of which is of blue enamel adorned by the thirteen stars. A helmet with visor closed, in light blue surmounts the shield." (See Fig. 7.)

The only other item in the same catalogue attributed to Thomas Jefferson is described as "A custard Stand of French porcelain decorated with detached bachelor's buttons." However, so many errors in attribution appear in the Lyon catalogue that it is difficult to accept this identification as a positive one.

Of other Jefferson plates, an octagonal dish of dark blue Rockingham ware stamped "Brameld" exists in the White House china collection. This plate was first described in 1892 by Alice Morse Earle in *China Collecting in America*. Mrs. Earle said that another plate was "sold at auction in New York, about fifteen years ago, which was catalogued as having been the property of Jefferson and used on his dinner table." The description of this plate is the same as the plate in the Lyon catalogue, which is obviously the auction Mrs. Earle refers to. This plate brought, according to Mrs. Earle, $40; the custard cup sold for $2.50.

Several pieces of the monogrammed china were given to the White House at the beginning of this century by descendants of Jefferson. This group consisted of a soup tureen and cover, the top of a vegetable dish, a large platter, and a plate. The Smithsonian Institution has no Jefferson china listed in its collection.

CHAPTER 5

James Madison
1809–1817

Thomas Jefferson had managed, during his term as President, to furnish at least twenty of the rooms in the mansion, so that when his protégés, the James Madisons, moved in, the house was respectable and comfortable. Dolley Madison had acted as hostess on occasion for Jefferson and was therefore practiced in the art of official entertaining when her husband took office in 1809. It was said of Dolley Madison that her table was her pride. The superabundance of dishes and their size were, however, subjects of ridicule to a foreign minister who observed, "It was more like a harvest-home supper, than the entertainment of a Secretary of State." (See Plates 7, 8.)

Dolley Madison, upon overhearing this remark, answered that "she thought abundance was preferable to elegance; that circumstances formed customs, and customs formed taste; and as to the profusion so repugnant to foreign customs, they arose from the happy circumstance of the superabundance and prosperity of our country, she did not hesitate to sacrifice the delicacy of European taste for the less elegant, but more liberal fashion of Virginia."

This philosophy of entertaining on a lavish scale was continued by the Madisons when they entered the White House. The vivacious personality and warmth of the First Lady were even more popular drawing cards for guests at the Executive Mansion.

The Madison administration was clouded by the second war with Britain, declared in 1812; and entertaining at the White House was interrupted after the British soldiers entered Washington in August of 1814 and set fire to the President's house. The unfortunate burning of the White House has been described often, and many legends concerning the historic flight of Dolley Madison in the wake of this event have been told. However, no story could be more accurate than the description written by the First Lady herself on the day of the occurrence, Tuesday, August 23, 1814, in a letter to her sister at Mount Vernon:

> Dear Sister: My husband left me yesterday morning to join General Winder. He inquired anxiously whether I had courage or firmness to remain in the President's House until his return, on the morrow or succeeding day, and on my assurance that I had no fear but for him and the success of our army, he left, beseeching me to take care of myself, and of Cabinet papers, public and private. I have since received two dispatches from him written with a pencil; the last is alarming, because he desires that I should be ready at a moment's warning to enter my carriage and leave the city; that the enemy seemed stronger than had been reported, and that it might happen that they would reach the city with intention to destroy it, . . . I am accordingly ready; I have pressed as many Cabinet papers into trunks as to fill one carriage; our private property must be sacrificed, as it is impossible to procure wagons for its transportation. I am determined not to go myself, until I see Mr. Madison safe and he can accompany me, . . . as I hear of much hostility toward him. . . . Disaffection stalks around us. . . . My friends and acquaintances are all gone, even Colonel C., with his hundred men, who are stationed as a guard in this enclosure. . . .
>
> Wednesday morning, twelve o'clock. . . . Since sunrise I have been turning my spy-glass in every direction and watching with unwearied anxiety, hoping to discover the approach of my dear husband and his friends; but alas! I can descry only groups of military wandering in all directions, as if there was a lack of arms, or of spirits, to fight for their own firesides!
>
> Three o'clock. . . . Will you believe it, my sister? We have had a battle or skirmish near Bladensburgh, and I am still here within the sound of the cannon! Mr. Madison comes not; may God protect him! Two messen-

gers covered with dust come to bid me fly; but I wait for him. . . . At this late hour a wagon has been procured; I have had it filled with the plate and most valuable portable articles belonging to the house; whether it will reach its destination, the Bank of Maryland, or fall into the hands of British soldiery, events must determine. Our kind friend, Mr. Carroll, has come to hasten my departure, and is in a very bad humor with me because I insist on waiting until the large picture of General Washington is secured, and it requires to be unscrewed from the wall. This process was found too tedious for these perilous moments; I have ordered the frame to be broken and the canvas taken out; it is done . . . and the precious portrait placed in the hands of two gentlemen from New York for safe keeping.

Soon after Mrs. Madison's flight, the President returned to the mansion with a party of soldiers. It is said that after the Presidential party left, vagrant soldiers wandered about the house and grounds, which had been left in the hands of a few servants who were unable to control the uninvited guests. Many articles were probably removed from the house during this period, some perhaps to be secured and returned, others never to be restored. Although the major portion of Madison belongings were undoubtedly stolen or burned by British soldiers, other objects were certainly removed beforehand by servants and ransackers.

Alice Morse Earle dismisses the existence of Madison china by saying that the official china was destroyed at the burning of the Executive Mansion by the British. It is the romance of the story that has caused collectors and dealers and even experts at the Smithsonian Institution and the White House to attribute a large centerpiece to the Madison administration. More recently, the large porcelain piece has been assigned to the Jackson administration, despite earlier legends that have Mrs. Madison packing it in her wagon and carrying it off. More current information dates this controversial bowl later than Jackson, and it and the matching plates in existence will be discussed in Chapter 16.

Three days after the burning of their home, the Madisons returned to Washington and shortly after moved into Octagon House, formerly the home of the French minister. Dolley Madison resumed her position as hostess at this location until she moved to a house on the corner of Pennsylvania Avenue and Nineteenth Street. It was here that the Madison term was ended—in a sparsely furnished house, with remnants of glass, china, earthenware, and linens with which to

Fig. 8   Dark blue and gold serving dish once owned by James Madison. The remaining three plates are from state dinner servic Madison administration. (*The Smithsonian Institution*)

entertain. Even here, spectacular parties were held, attended by all the elite of Washington. (See Plate 9.)

It is probable that the remaining china attributed to the Madison era dates from the Madisons' move to this house. There are a few pieces of French china in existence that are said to have belonged to Dolley Madison. The pattern is a border of deep buff decorated with a series of wheel patterns outlined in black. A small serving dish, belonging to the Smithsonian Institution, is dark blue and gold. Remnants of a tea set, also attributed to the Madisons, are pale blue, gold, and white. However, these attributions are more traditional than positive. (See Fig. 8.)

CHAPTER 6

James Monroe
1817–1825

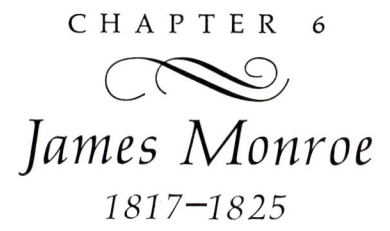

James Monroe and his First Lady moved into the Executive Mansion under less than ideal conditions. The White House possessed few comforts and no elegance, and the debris of the burned building still lay in heaps about the grounds. Work on the house had been started in the spring of 1815 in the hope that it would be ready for occupancy by the time of Monroe's inauguration in 1817, but it was yet a while before the mansion was habitable. The day before the inauguration, Congress appropriated $20,000 so that new furniture, plate, china, and glass could be purchased.

President Monroe, having served many years in France, had great affection for that country and its style and manners. He understood the historical and monetary value of the furnishings he chose, and on February 12, 1818, he wrote a message asking for government supervision for the furnishings in the Executive Mansion so that the objects he purchased with such care would be preserved:

> All the public furniture provided before 1814 having been destroyed with the public buildings in that year, and little afterwards procured owing to the inadequacy of the appropriation, it has become necessary to provide almost every article requisite for such an establishment: Whence

the sum expended will be much greater than any former period. The furniture in its kind and extent, is thought to be an object not less deserving attention than the building for which it is intended. But being national objects, each seems to have an equal claim to legislative sanction. The disbursement of the public money, too, ought, it is presumed, be in like manner provided for by law. The person who may happen to be placed, by the suffrage of his fellow-citizens, in this high trust, having no personal interest in these concerns, should be exempted from undue responsibility respecting them.

For a building so extensive, intended for a purpose exclusively national, in which, in the furniture provided for it, a mingled regard is due to the simplicity and purity of our institutions, and to the character of the people who are represented in it, the sum already appropriated has proved altogether inadequate. The present is, therefore, a proper time for Congress to take the subject into consideration, with a view to all the objects claiming attention, and to regulate it by law. On a knowledge of the furniture procured, and the sum expended for it, a just estimate may be formed, regarding the extent of the building, of what will still be wanted to furnish the House. Many of the articles being of a durable nature, may be handed down through a long series of service; and being of great value, such as plate, ought not to be left altogether, and at all times, to the care of servants alone. It seems to be advisable that a public agent should be charged with it during the occasional absences of the President, and have authority to transfer it from one President to another, and likewise to make reports of occasional deficiencies, as the basis on this further provision should be made.

Had Congress only listened to Monroe, life in the White House would have been somewhat less complicated for succeeding First Families. Until recently, little historical value was placed on White House furnishings, and perhaps the objects thought to be of the least value were parts of dinner or dessert services remaining from previous administrations. (See Plates 1, 2.)

Monroe's own china and furniture, gathered during his many years of service in France, were purchased by the government for a sum of $9,071.22½. Federal appraisers set the price of the various objects that came from the Monroes' Washington house. Additional furnishings and a porcelain dessert service were ordered from France in an attempt to equip the White House with sufficient articles for the formal entertaining required of the President. (See Plate 9.)

The one object ordered from France by Monroe which has graced the table in the State Dining Room more times than any other decorative object is the elegant *surtout de table*, a centerpiece composed of seven mirrors that may be made shorter by the removal of some of the sections. The centerpiece has a gallery of bronze gilt along which are placed sixteen figures holding a crown in either hand. The crowns may be used as rings in which small cups are placed to hold candles or flowers. Additional baskets, tripods, and candelabra complete this elaborate table furniture. The Monroe plateau has been, throughout the history of the White House, the one decorative object to which the fewest First Ladies objected, and it has been used often. Many of the Sèvres vases, bronze clocks, and other mantel and table ornaments still in use at the White House were also purchased by James Monroe. (See Fig. 9.)

Entertainment at the Executive Mansion during the earlier part of the Monroe administration was not as open nor as enjoyable as it had been under the popular Dolley Madison. Mrs. Monroe was a retiring woman whose many years in France had given her some delusions of grandeur. She began her years as First Lady by antagonizing Washington society. She refused to return calls and made it a practice never to make first calls, a tradition around which the entire social life of Washington revolved. Subsequent First Ladies undoubtedly have blessed Mrs. Monroe for having had the courage to break this tradition, but Elizabeth Monroe suffered many snubs, and her earliest entertainments were boycotted by the ladies whose homes she had refused to grace with her presence.

Mrs. Monroe seemed to have been the exact opposite of the flamboyant and popular Dolley Madison. Dolley Madison, called by contemporary newswriters "the most popular woman in the United States," was a difficult act to follow in any case, although Mrs. Monroe did not seem inclined to try. A great deal of public resentment followed Monroe's extravagant purchases of furnishings, not the least of which was the *surtout*, which had cost 6,000 francs.

The Monroes' dinners were formal and fashioned after those they had attended and given in France. The food and the table service were French, also. James Fenimore Cooper, a guest at the President's house during the Monroe administration, wrote of one Monroe dinner: "On this occasion we were honored with the presence of Mrs. Monroe, and two or three of her female relatives.

Crossing the hall we were admitted to the drawing room, in which most of the company were already assembled. The hour was six. By far the greater part of the guests were men, and perhaps two-thirds were members of Congress."

If one reads between the lines of Mr. Cooper's description, it is possible to find the attitude of Washington society toward Elizabeth Monroe. The Congressmen came because they had to, but their wives did not. Mrs. Monroe's relatives were the only ladies she could count on to be present.

Cooper further describes his evening:

> There was a great gravity of mien in most of the company, and neither any very marked exhibition nor any positively striking want, of grace or manner. The conversation was commonplace, and a little sombre, though two or three men of the world got around the ladies, where the battle of words was maintained with sufficient spirit. . . . To me the entertainment had a rather formal air. When dinner was announced, the oldest Senator present took Mrs. Monroe and led her to the table. The rest of the party followed without much order. The President took a lady, as usual, and preceded the rest of the guests. . . .
>
> The dining-room was in better taste than is common here, being quite simple and but little furnished. The table was large and rather handsome. The service was in china, as is uniformly the case, plate being exceedingly rare, if at all used. There was, however, a rich plateau, and a great abundance of the smaller articles of table plate. The cloth, napkins &c., &c., were fine and beautiful.
>
> The dinner was served in the French style, a little Americanized. The dishes were handed around, though some of the guests, appearing to prefer their own customs, coolly helped themselves to what they found at hand.

The Monroe dinners started at six o'clock and ended around nine. Previously, a social evening in the White House began at four in the afternoon. Although Mrs. Monroe may have been criticized for her aloof manners, she was obviously not afraid of this criticism and established innovations in White House protocol that have lasted to this day.

Much of Washington indulged in a favorite pastime of criticizing the First Lady, but others found qualities of which they could approve. In the latter part of the Monroe administration, Eliza Hayes, Monroe's daughter, substituted for her mother at many of the social functions held in the city. By this time, it had become apparent to other members of the governmental body that they needed the prestige of White House social life far more than the Monroes needed them, and attendance improved. This minor Monroe social doctrine did appeal to French and British diplomats, who were accustomed to heads of state being set above and apart.

James and Elizabeth Monroe, before their tenure in the Executive Mansion, had been used to the best, and at that time the "best" in the decorative arts was French. In the vouchers found in the National Archives is a description of the

Fig. 9   Drawing from 1908 article showing Monroe state dinner pattern on left. (*From The Century Magazine, October, 1908. Drawing by Harry Fenn. Photograph by Charles Klamkin.*)

forty-one packages ordered by Monroe from France, including "a dessert service made by Dagoty, with amaranth border and five vignettes representing Strength, Agriculture, Commerce, Art and Science with Arms of the United States in center." This porcelain service had settings for thirty people, and many other plates were included in the same order. Another Monroe pattern is described as carrying a dainty scroll in red, blue, and gold; an odd plate (in the White House China Room) has a dull orange rim in flat tones broken at the edge by six groups of white leaves; the center bears a bunch of flowers.

The Dagoty service is generally considered the Monroe state service because it can definitely be attributed and bears a patriotic motif. Also, it was paid for with government funds. However, many other plates have been attributed to the Monroe era, some of which were purchased in France by the Monroes while they were there and which were later sold to the government.

Fig. 10   Plate from White House china used during administration of President James Monroe. (*The Smithsonian Institution-Loan of Mr. L. G. Hoes.*)

None of the Dagoty service remained consistently in the White House, regardless of Monroe's early warnings to Congress. White House and Smithsonian historians can only be grateful to private collectors for preserving the examples of the Monroe china that do exist today. In 1958, only one soup plate from the Dagoty service was in possession of the government, and it was placed in the White House collection at that time. There was no example of the pattern in the Smithsonian collection. It is said that Mrs. Kennedy was responsible for the loan of a plate to each of the collections from the Henry Francis du Pont Winterthur Museum in Delaware. These loans were made permanent upon the death of Mr. Henry Francis du Pont.

The two pieces of the Dagoty service illustrated on Plate 9 have never before been photographed, and it is through a study of the serving pieces that we can more easily visualize the Monroe table set for state dinners. Although historians may find fault with the Monroes' sociability, no one can quarrel with James and Elizabeth Monroe's good taste.

CHAPTER 7

John Quincy Adams
1825–1829

By the time John Quincy Adams and his wife, Louisa, moved into the White House, they had already experienced many arduous years in the service of their country. Adams and his wife had lived in Germany, Russia, and London; and the difficult years Louisa Adams had spent in Russia had taken their toll. The two older Adams boys were left at home with their grandparents and did not see their mother for six years. Another child, a daughter, was born in Russia and did not live long.

Adams had been elected President by a narrow majority over the popular Andrew Jackson, and the pair never seemed quite at ease in their tenuous positions as President and First Lady. Although the customary levees, receptions, and dinners were held, neither of the Adamses seemed to have enjoyed them. Probably their most outstanding house guest was General Lafayette who spent the last weeks of his American tour at the Executive Mansion.

Mrs. Adams, an educated and accomplished woman, was in poor health from the beginning of her husband's administration. Even so, she performed her duties as hostess as well as she was able and managed to furnish the East Room of the

White House with French objects which, although they brought little criticism to Monroe, became bait for Adams's enemies during his administration.

Shortly after Adams became President, he made an inventory of all the equipment he found in the mansion. There were 270 pieces of the Monroe dinner service left. Of the crimson and gold dessert service, Adams found only 157 pieces remaining. This inventory included "four elegant ice cream urns." This Monroe china was used as the state china during John Quincy Adams's administration.

A Meissen plate that exists in the White House china collection represents the Adamses' years spent abroad. The plate is decorated with a large rosette in the center, and the rim has five small panels of pale lavender outlined in gold. Each panel encloses two white figures that resemble seahorses. Another Meissen plate, in the popular Onion pattern, is attributed to the Adams household and is on display at the Smithsonian Institution. It is probable that both of these services were brought to the White House and used during the Adamses' four years. (See Plates 10, 11.)

There is little question that neither of the two Adamses was unhappy when their term of occupancy in the Executive Mansion was over. Writing of the First Lady in 1880, Laura C. Holloway, in her book *The Ladies of the White House or, In the Home of the Presidents*, said: "Mrs. Adams retired from the White House with heartfelt pleasure, and sought the quiet her delicate health demanded."

CHAPTER 8

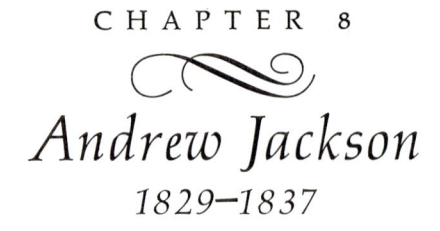

Andrew Jackson
1829–1837

The peace and quiet of the Adams administration was a strong contrast to the rowdyism of the Jackson years in the White House. Jackson's inaugural reception is probably more legend than fact at this date, but several journalists recorded at the time that the ebullient atmosphere and general unruliness of Jackson's admirers made short work of what was left of the Monroe china and glassware on this occasion. It was reported that "china and glass to the amount of several thousand dollars were broken in the struggle to get at the ices and cakes."

During the John Quincy Adams administration, Congress had passed a measure requiring that all furnishings for the White House be of domestic origin. In so far as it was possible, succeeding Presidents did attempt to comply with this ruling. However, it would be many years before American potters could supply good-quality dinner services in sufficient quantity for White House needs.

Therefore, Jackson, like his predecessors, ordered his state china from France. The order was placed through an American agent, Lewis Veron, of Philadelphia. Patriotic as Jackson was, suitable American china simply was not available. The French dinner service, decorated with the American eagle, was made to order for Jackson and consisted of 440 pieces. Another dinner and dessert service, of sterling silver, was made for Jackson in France at a cost of $4,308.82. This "people's President" obviously intended to live in a manner more regal than any President before him.

Jackson began his term of office in deep sorrow. His wife, Rachel, to whom he was devoted, died on December 23, before Jackson's inauguration. Her oft-quoted comment, made shortly before her death, reflected her attitude toward her husband's office. She had said, "I assure you that I would rather be a door-keeper in the house of my God, than to live in that Palace in Washington."

If the White House was not a "Palace" before Jackson's occupancy, it closely resembled one soon after. Fifty thousand dollars was spent refurnishing the mansion. Gilt chandeliers, new furniture for the East Room, gilded tables, Brussels carpeting, silk upholstery, and great mirrors were purchased to make the interior of the building as palatial as possible. It is highly probable that Jackson's pipe-smoking Rachel would not have been happy in those surroundings after all.

Andrew Jackson, however, was not without his hostesses, who presided at the large parties he gave during his two terms of office. Mrs. Emily Donelson, the wife of Mrs. Jackson's nephew, became the official hostess of the President's house during the Jackson administration. Her husband served as Jackson's secretary. In addition, Jackson's foster son's wife, Sarah Yorke Jackson, also served as hostess at the White House and later was mistress of The Hermitage, Jackson's home.

The Jackson White House was constantly filled with young people. Having had no children of their own, the Jacksons acted as foster parents for a dozen children. The first baby to be born in the White House in that administration was the child of Sarah Yorke Jackson and Andrew Jackson, Jr., the adopted son whose poor financial judgment was to plague Jackson until the day he died. When the baby was born, Jackson issued a blanket invitation to all official Washington to attend the christening. Congress adjourned so that members could join in the celebration. In later years, this baby was the donor of the Jackson display of glassware, china, and silver plate to the White House collection.

The porcelain punch bowl illustrated in this chapter is probably one of the most interesting existing relics from the Jackson administration. The decoration on this bowl commemorates two weddings that took place in the White House in the same year, 1832. The first wedding, of Mary Ann Eastin to Lucius Junius Polk, was held on April 10. The second wedding, of Mary Ann Lewis, to Alphonse Pageot, occurred on November 29.

Lucius Polk was the third son of Colonel William Polk and a cousin of President Polk. He was from Columbia, Tennessee, and had met Mary Ann Eastin at a party at The Hermitage, Jackson's home. Miss Eastin had fallen in love with another man, but Polk, with Jackson's encouragement, won her from her suitor. Andrew Jackson disapproved of the first choice, and he advised Miss Eastin to take her time and to consider Mr. Polk as a possibility for a suitable husband. He advised her, "Take care, my dear; with love, marriage is heaven, without it, hell."

Jackson, obviously feeling somewhat responsible for the Eastin-Polk match, paid for their wedding. Miss Eastin was, at the time, along with many others, a resident of the White House. The Jackson and Polk families had been close for many years. The wedding was the first to be held in the East Room.

Alphonse Pageot was a member of the French Legation when he met Mary Ann Lewis. She was the daughter of Major William Berkely Lewis, a member of Jackson's Kitchen Cabinet. Lewis and Jackson had been neighbors in Tennessee and had served many years in the army together. The Lewises also lived in the White House. Andrew Jackson, ever generous, paid for the Pageot wedding, too, although the expense of the Eastin-Polk wedding made it necessary for the second Mary Ann to have a somewhat smaller celebration. Only the cabinet, the diplomatic corps, the Supreme Court justices, and assorted friends and relatives were invited.

The punch bowl that commemorates these two White House weddings might possibly have been a gift to Jackson from the French Legation. It is Paris porcelain. The front and back are hand-decorated with two full-blown roses. On either side of the center roses are smaller blossoms with cherubs. In each of the two large center roses are portraits of the two Mary Anns. The American eagle is painted on the two opposite sides. (See Plates 3, 12.)

It is seldom one sees a relic of the White House that is as easily attributable as the Jackson punch bowl. Most certainly it expresses Jackson's sentiments toward these two young couples who, by being married in the White House, were given an important place in American history.

CHAPTER 9

Martin Van Buren
1837–1841

The hospitality and open-door policy of Andrew Jackson were particularly unappealing to his successor, Martin Van Buren. The expensive furnishings that had been purchased by Jackson were ruined during eight years of generous entertaining, and the final damage had been done by the hordes of Jackson worshippers who descended on the building for one farewell debacle where uncontrolled mobs ground food into the damask and the Brussels carpeting.

Van Buren cleared out the mess left by the Jackson crowd, and Congress gave the new President $27,000 to purchase new furniture and tableware once the broken Jackson pieces were gotten rid of. In contrast to Jackson's wild inaugural, Van Buren did not open the White House for a large reception until New Year's Day.

Van Buren was a fastidious man and had the reputation for being a *bon vivant*. His style of entertaining was formal, and he gave many small dinner parties where the eating and drinking could be confined to the dining room.

Mrs. Van Buren had died seventeen years before her husband became the eighth President of the United States, and when Van Buren took office in 1837, he had no one to act as official hostess. The following year, the President's oldest son married Angelica Singleton. Dolley Madison, still going strong as Washington's unofficial hostess, had introduced the two. Major Van Buren acted as his father's secretary, and his wife performed her first official duties as hostess the following New Year's Day. (See Plate 12.)

The nation's economy was in poor shape and grew even worse right after Van Buren became President. The enormous expenditures of the popular Jackson went unnoticed by the country, but Van Buren was not to be let off so easily. He ordered a set of blue, gold, and white china for the White House from France at a cost of $1,000. This purchase resulted in an arraignment before a congressional committee. It was not just the expense the Congress objected to, but the double crime of the President purchasing his china abroad. The state of ceramic art in America was still such that American porcelain was unavailable, but Congress chose to ignore this fact.

The member of Congress from Pennsylvania, a Mr. Ogle, led the attack on Van Buren's extravagance by exclaiming that the White House "looked like a Court Banqueting Room resembling in style and magnificence the banqueting halls of Oriental Monarchs!" Ogle described the 440-piece dinner service and matching dessert service as consisting of "sixty Greek form cups and saucers, six stands for bon bons, six tambours, twelve compotiers on feet, six huge fruit baskets on feet, four ice cream vases and covers with inside bowls, and numerous other useless and extravagant vessels."

Van Buren was accused of maintaining a "royal establishment" and a "palace as splendid as that of the Caesars and as richly adorned as the proudest Asiatic mansion." Another transgression for which Congress would not forgive Van Buren was the expenditure of $75 to have the Monroe *surtout de table* repaired. It, too, had suffered from Jacksonian neglect.

It was a matter of necessity that Van Buren made the effort, against much abuse and argument, to refurbish the Executive Mansion. The rough treatment the building and its appointments had suffered under Old Hickory had left it with threadbare carpets and broken china. Van Buren ordered quantities of "blue-edged dishes, blue printed plates, gold-band china coffees, willow plates and dishes." From the description, one would assume that this lot was ordinary earthenware of the type then being used in many middle-class households in America.

Van Buren's purported extravagance was used as a political issue in the 1840 campaign, and much was made of his expenditures. The Harrison-Tyler campaign was aggressive and involved much name-calling. "Van, Van's a used up man" was a refrain called across the country. After the verbal beating Van Buren had taken from the very congressmen who had sat down to his carefully planned and genteelly served meals, Van Buren could not have been too unhappy to take up residence once again in his home state of New York.

CHAPTER 10

William Henry Harrison
1841

William Henry Harrison did not occupy the White House long enough to have ordered china or, for that matter, much of anything else. As difficult as the campaign of 1840 had been for Martin Van Buren, it really took its toll on the Presidential winner. The vigorous campaign during a period of economic depression exhausted the old soldier, and he died after holding office for just one month.

Anna Symes Harrison did not get to the White House at all. She had vigorously protested Harrison's nomination for President four years earlier and disapproved even more the second time around. Put in the polite nineteenth-century language of author Laura C. Holloway, "She was grateful to her countrymen for this unmistakable appreciation of the civil and military services of her husband, and rejoiced at his vindication over his traducers, but she took no pleasure in contemplating the pomp and circumstance of a life at the Executive Mansion."

Another statement of Mrs. Holloway's might suffice in summing up Harrison's short term of office. "Pneumonia was the avowed cause [of death], but it was the applicants for office who killed him."

The White House china collection has a luster pitcher to commemorate Harrison's term. Like many household articles of 1840, this pitcher has a print of a log cabin, representing the phrase that boomeranged on Harrison's opposition during the campaign. Harrison, wanting to be known as a people's candidate, played up his state of poverty by claiming he had lived in a log cabin, which was not true. A news writer sneeringly retorted, "Give him a barrel of cider, and settle a pension of two thousand a year on him, and my word for it he will sit the remainder of his days in his log cabin." It was not long before the log-cabin motif appeared on every item from bandannas to whisky bottles. A great many plates and jugs were also printed with this motif. (See Plate 12.)

CHAPTER 11

John Tyler
1841–1845

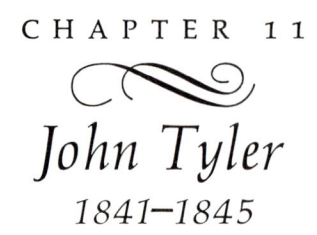

John Tyler was the first vice-president to be called upon to take over the office of Chief Administrator. His wife was in delicate health when she came to live in the White House. A letter written by her son, Major Robert Tyler, best describes the social life of the White House during the Tyler administration.

> My mother's health was entirely too delicate to permit her to charge herself with the semi-official social requirements of the mansion, and my married sisters being absent for most of the time, the task devolved upon Mrs. Robert Tyler to represent my mother on stated occasions. . . . During my mother's life, and up to this date, always contemning pretension and worldly vanity, we lived in the "White house" as we lived at home, save that we were obliged to have more company, but less select as to true worth than was altogether agreeable. In the course of the "fashionable season," and while the sessions of the Congress lasted, we gave two dinner parties each week, very much after the plain, substantial Virginia manner and style, to the first of which, usually confined to gentlemen from different parts of the country visiting Washington, and who had shown respectful attention to the President and family, twenty guests were always invited; and to the second, usually embracing both ladies and gentlemen from among the dignitaries of the different departments of

the Federal and State governments, and the diplomatic corps of foreign governments, forty persons were invited, making in either case quite a full table.

In addition to the dinner parties mentioned, the drawing rooms of the White House were opened every evening until ten oclock; private balls were held; and every Saturday evening in the summer, the general public was invited to concerts on the grounds at the south front of the mansion. On January 1 and the Fourth of July, similar entertainments for the public were held. However, Robert Tyler goes on to complain, "Such was the bitterness of party feeling toward us, that no appropriation was made by Congress either for furnishing the house or for the office of private secretary, or for the incidental expenses of fuel, lights, door-keepers, messengers, &c., that are now [1880] so abundant as really to double the salary of the Executive Office over what it was then."

It is little wonder that Tyler did not purchase state china during his administration. (See Plate 13.)

The first Mrs. Tyler died on September 10, 1842; and two years later, on June 26, 1844, Tyler married Miss Julia Gardiner, who was thirty years the President's junior. Julia Gardiner Tyler, brought up on what could have passed for a kingdom in America, a private island off Long Island, used the eight months remaining to her in Washington to reign supreme as mistress of the White House. She received her guests while seated on a thronelike chair and was attended by "maids of honor" who stood on either side. Julia Tyler's farewell to Washington was a formal ball for 2,000 guests.

Representing the Tyler administration in the White House china collection is a dinner plate with a chocolate-colored center against which is painted a bunch of nasturtiums. The border is of wheat painted in gold.

CHAPTER 12

James Knox Polk
1845–1849

Whatever else might be said of the Polk administration, no one can accuse it of having been lively. The final extravagant gala of Julia Tyler would have to last the elite of Washington a good while. Sarah Childress Polk, a product of the Moravian Institute of Salem, North Carolina, had had a disciplined upbringing; and she brought a sense of order and, many said, boredom to the Capitol.

Mrs. Polk refused to serve refreshments at the public receptions at the White House, and for the first time, police guards attended the functions as protection for the First Family. Mrs. Polk was a staunch Presbyterian, and she felt that the position of the Presidency should be dignified and subdued. She did away with cardplaying and dancing in the Executive Mansion and received her guests while seated in a chair.

A visitor to the White House during the Polk administration described the First Lady: "Unlike some of her predecessors, Mrs. Polk has no taste for the gay amusements of the lovers of pleasure."

Obviously believing that cleanliness was second only to godliness, Mrs. Polk made much of the sorry state of the White House and cleaned out all broken furniture and dishes. Lacking enough funds to replace White House china on a grand scale, she brought in some of her own plates and ordered a small supplementary service for state use. The Polk china is the first White House china on which a shield of red, white, and blue can be found.

A lattice-work compote of Dresden china in the White House china collection has a decoration of vignettes of birds in plumage. Several matching pieces with a pink and gold border and sprays of violet morning glories also represent the Polk administration. (See Fig. 11.)

The Polk state china with the United States shield has a shaped, molded, and scrolled gilt rim with the shield just below the border. Some of the plates have flowers painted in the center and a colored border; others, probably the dessert plates, have a gold scroll in the center. The plates are marked: "Ed Honoré / Boul^d Poissonnière No 15 / à Paris / Manufacture / à Champeaux à Paris / No / Prix." (See Plates 13, 14.)

The Polk administration was not known for its lavish entertainments, but Mrs. Polk was highly praised by her mid-nineteenth-century contemporaries. Earlier Presidents had spent their lifetime fortunes while in the White House. The parsimonious Polks were the first to leave Washington with money put aside from the President's salary.

Fig. 11 Drawing made in 1908 of fruit basket and cup and saucer from Polk china in White House collection. (*From The Century Magazine, October, 1908. Engraving by Harry Fenn. Photograph by Charles Klamkin.*)

CHAPTER 13

Zachary Taylor
1849–1850

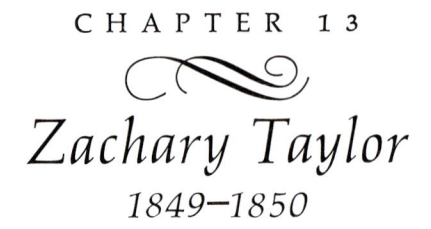

Margaret Taylor, the wife of our twelfth President, "saw nothing attractive in the surroundings of the White House." She opposed her husband becoming a candidate and explained to friends who spoke of him being elected President, "That it was a plot to deprive her of his society, and shorten his life by unnecessary care and responsibility...."

Mrs. Taylor refused to accept any obligation of official receptions, and her daughter, Elizabeth, who was twenty-two at the time, became the official White House hostess. It was said that "Mrs. Taylor was never visible in the reception-room; she received her visitors in her private apartments, and escaped all observation from choice. Once established in her new home, she selected such rooms as suited her ideas of housekeeping, and, as far as was possible, resumed the routine that characterized her life at Baton Rouge."

Few official receptions were given. It was soon understood that set, formal, and official dinners were not coveted, and they most certainly were not encouraged. Afternoon teas were hostessed by Betty Bliss, the Taylors' daughter, and dancing and drinking were not allowed any more than they had been in the Polk administration.

Mrs. Taylor did not have to withstand the tortures of the White House long. Her husband died after being in office a little more than a year. It was said that from the time Mrs. Taylor left the White House, she never alluded to her residence there, except as connected to the death of her husband.

The Taylor administration is represented in the White House china collection by a blue Staffordshire platter and a green vegetable dish made by British potters. A blue and white Canton soup plate is also a Taylor relic. (See Plate 4.)

CHAPTER 14

Millard Fillmore
1850–1853

When Zachary Taylor died, some said it was a result of having eaten too many cherries and having consumed too much ice water. Others attributed the death to typhoid fever. Some newspapers blamed the death on the unhealthy conditions that prevailed in the White House. The cellars were always damp, and the Potomac River rose up on the south lawns. There were rumors that Millard Fillmore had refused to move into the house.

Congress appropriated money for a renovation of the mansion, and one of Fillmore's first purchases was a coal stove for the kitchen. All cooking had previously been done in the huge fireplace.

Mrs. Fillmore did not move to Washington from her home in Buffalo when her husband became vice-president. However, she did join him in the White House after Taylor's death. She was an educated woman and bemoaned the fact that there was no library in the Executive Mansion. Congress appropriated money for her to purchase books.

Abigail Fillmore, older than her husband and already ailing when she moved to Washington, had her daughter, Mary Abigail, act as assistant hostess. The eighteen-year-old girl was an accomplished musician who spoke French fluently.

She removed the burden of entertaining from her mother's shoulders as often as she could.

White House entertaining did go on, though in the lackluster manner of the Polks; and Mrs. Fillmore did manage, even with an injured ankle, to stand in receiving lines for hours. Dinner parties, Friday night levees, and Tuesday morning receptions were held during the congressional season. Toward the end of her husband's administration, Mrs. Fillmore was seen less and less. She lived only one month beyond Fillmore's term of office.

Shortly after the death of President Fillmore, in 1874, Mrs. E. Terry and her sister, Miss Cornelia Burtis, purchased the Fillmore residence in Buffalo. Many of Fillmore's personal belongings were included in the sale. Among them were three pieces of blue and white Staffordshire earthenware that were presented to the White House china collection in 1909.

CHAPTER 15

Franklin Pierce
1853–1857

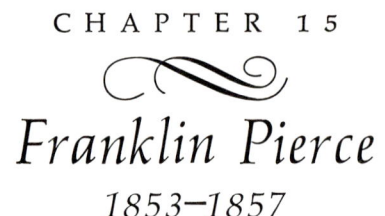

Jane Appleton Pierce did not enjoy the social life of Washington any more than did her immediate predecessors in the White House. She had had a childhood "fragile and drooping in health" and was "inclined to pensive melancholy." She was described by Mrs. Holloway as being one of those persons who is "happier by far on the day of their deaths than during the years of their lives."

Tragedy did seem to stalk Mrs. Pierce. She coped during her married life with problems that would have tried a stronger woman. The Pierces had three sons and had lost two in death before Pierce was nominated for the Presidency. A final blow came when the third son was killed in a train wreck on the fifth of January before Pierce's inauguration. The parents were on the same train and survived the accident. Jane Pierce did not come to the White House in a party-giving frame of mind. In addition to the loss of three children, Mrs. Pierce had another sorrow to contend with; it is rumored throughout contemporary literature that President Pierce drank a lot.

There seems to be some discrepancy among Mrs. Pierce's biographers about whether the First Lady was present at the White House entertainments. One says, "She presided, too, with the President at the State dinners, as well as those

PLATE 13

Above Green-bordered French porcelain dessert plate with flower center from state china of James Knox Polk. Marked "E. D. Honoré." (*White House Historical Association. Photograph by National Geographic Society.*)

Left Blue and gold porcelain base with bisque kneeling figures supports a gilt fruit basket from the Tyler administration. It was presented to the White House by family descendants. (*White House Historical Association. Photograph by National Geographic Society.*)

Below Another plate from Polk dessert service and reverse, showing mark. (*The Smithsonian Institution*)

PLATE 14

Above Several pieces of Franklin Pierce state china made by Haviland. (*The Smithsonian Institution*)

Left White French porcelain dessert plate with mauve-pink border decorated with vignettes of birds. Used by President Polk in White House. (*The Smithsonian Institution*)

Below left White and gold dinner plate from Polk state dinner service. (*Private collection. Photograph by Charles Klamkin.*)

Below Small plate from Franklin Pierce red-edged Haviland china. (*Collection of Marjorie W. Hardy. Photograph by Charles Klamkin.*)

PLATE 15

Above Haviland plate, exactly as shown in exhibition engraving, except that it does not have President's monogram in shield. Plate of same set below. (Collection of Marjorie W. Hardy. Photograph by Charles Klamkin.)

Left Centerpiece from Haviland dessert service, historically attributed to President Madison or President Jackson, is from Crystal Palace design and therefore cannot have been made at an earlier date. (White House Historical Association. Photograph by National Geographic Society.)

Below Footed compote from disputed Haviland service. Heavy gilding decorates outside of bowl. (Private collection. Photograph by Charles Klamkin.)

Above Chipped Buchanan plate showing depth of glaze typical [of] white china made by Haviland at mid-century. As reported by [ea]rly writers on Presidential china, the porcelain is heavy. This [is] one reason it was thought by some to have been of Chinese [m]anufacture. (Private collection. Photograph by Charles Klamkin.)

Above Interior of compote, showing same decoration and shield in center as found on plates and centerpiece. (Private collection. Photograph by Charles Klamkin.)

PLATE 16

Left French porcelain covered cup from Lincoln buff-edged dinner service. (*Collection of Marjorie W. Hardy. Photograph by Charles Klamkin.*)

Below Plate, compote, and small platter from Abraham Lincoln state dinner service. Lincoln china was made by Haviland. (*The Smithsonian Institution*)

Right Plate and gravy boat with underdish from Lincoln buff-bordered dinner service. (*The Smithsonian Institution*)

PLATE 17

Above Odd-shaped serving plate from buff-edged dinner service purchased by Mary Todd Lincoln. (*Collection of Marjorie W. Hardy. Photograph by Charles Klamkin.*)

Right Staffordshire earthenware plate said to have belonged to Andrew Johnson and used in White House during his administration. Two-color printing was in common use for plate decoration in the second part of the nineteenth century. This was a stock pattern made for the American market. (*Collection of Marjorie W. Hardy. Photograph by Charles Klamkin.*)

Below Rose-bordered plate from Stanton dinner service said to have been used by the Grants in the White House before their state china was delivered. (*Collection of Marjorie W. Hardy. Photograph by Charles Klamkin.*)

Below Royal Worcester plate used by Lincoln at Summer White House at Soldier's Home, Washington, D.C. (*The Smithsonian Institution*)

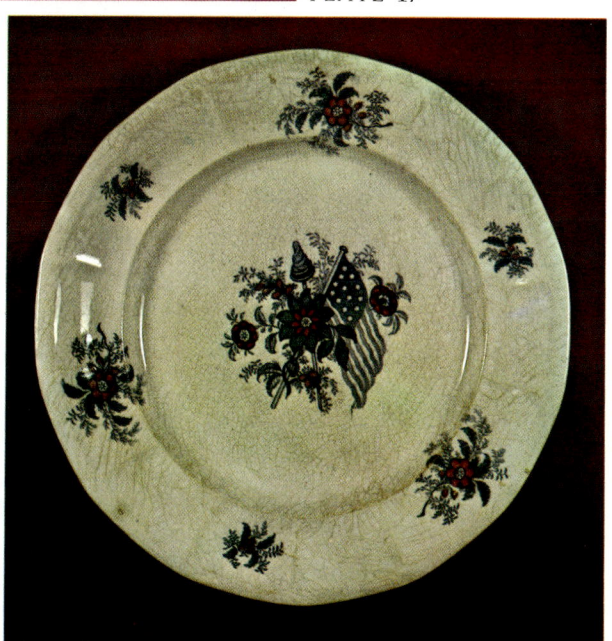

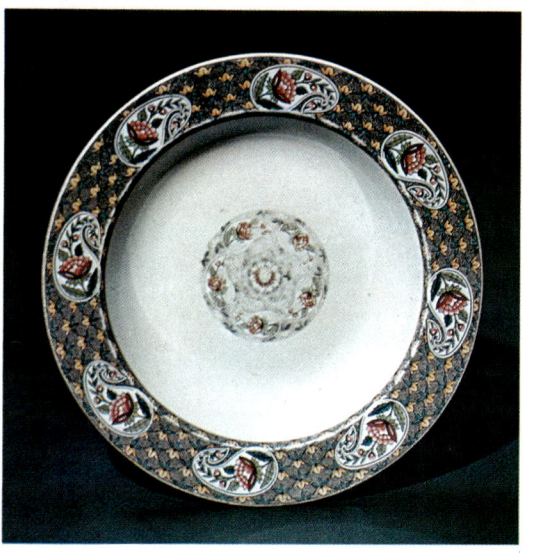

PLATE

Above Dinner plate from Grant state dinner service. Floral decoration is the carnation, Grant's state flower (Ohio). (Collection of Marjorie W. Hardy. Photograph by Charles Klamkin.)

Above Grant dinner plate with tulip as decoration. (Private collection. Photograph by Charles Klamkin.)

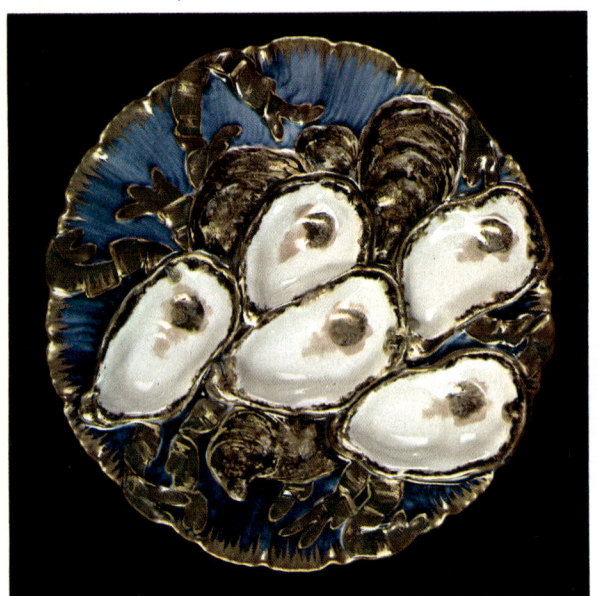

Above left Of this oyster plate from the Hayes service, Haviland said, "T rich effect of the design is enhanced by the method adapted in its manufactur The colors are laid upon the china clay under the glaze. China, color and gla are fired at the same time, producing an effect and integrity of color which pleasant to the eye and as durable as the porcelain itself." (Private collectio Photograph by Charles Klamkin.)

Above Reverse of oyster plate, showing incredible finish and marks. Almo all Hayes plates are dated, making it somewhat simpler to distinguish the repr ductions from the White House service. However, contrary to several ear writers' opinions, all seem to be of the same quality. (Private collection. Phot graph by Charles Klamkin.)

Left Soup plate from Hayes state dinner service. This "Green Turtle" so bowl, designed by Theodore Davis, was given special notice in the *Lond Times*, which said, "The green turtle is on a Florida reef, crawling between t ribs of an old wreck which is stranded. The moon is shedding a mellow lig which tinges the waves, and the moss on the wreck and the phosphorescence the waves give life to the drawing." (Collection of Marjorie W. Hardy. Phot graph by Charles Klamkin.)

Top Left Entitled by the artist "American Soup of the XVth Century," this design represents an Indian reclining upon a ledge of rocks. He is boiling his dinner in a pothole carved in the rocks. (Collection of Marjorie W. Hardy. Photograph by Charles Klamkin.)

Top right Entitled "On the Plains at Night," this design came from a sketch drawn by Davis while he was with General Custer. (Private collection. Photograph by Charles Klamkin.)

Above left Soup plate from Hayes state service, showing side placement of eagle. (The Smithsonian Institution)

Middle left Reverse of Hayes soup plate, showing marks and unusual spoke design. (The Smithsonian Institution)

Below left Dessert plate, "Pecan," illustrates the Texas red, or fox, squirrel eating pecan nuts that are grown in Texas. (Collection of Marjorie W. Hardy. Photograph by Charles Klamkin.)

Below Hayes game plate entitled "Ptarmigan's Bath." The ptarmigan is found in the Rocky Mountains, and its plumage turns white in the winter. This plate is 9 inches in diameter. (Collection of Marjorie W. Hardy. Photograph by Charles Klamkin.)

PLATE 19

PLATE 20

Right "California Quail" is one of the twelve designs for "The Game Course" painted by Theodore Davis. (*Collection of Marjorie W. Hardy. Photograph by Charles Klamkin.*)

Middle left Turkey platter from Hayes dinner service that is part of White House collection of Presidential china. All shapes as well as decorations for this dinner service were designed by Theodore Davis. (*The Smithsonian Institution*)

Middle right Plate from "The Fish Series" designed for President and Mrs. Hayes by Davis. Lobster is depicted crawling out of the water. (*Collection of Marjorie W. Hardy. Photograph by Charles Klamkin.*)

Bottom Obverse and reverse of Hayes game plate, "Woodcock," designed by Theodore Davis for Haviland. (*The Smithsonian Institution*)

Fig. 12   Drawing of plates from Franklin Pierce red-edged dinner service made by Haviland. These pieces were in the White House collection of Presidential china in 1908. (*From The Century Magazine, October, 1908. Drawing by Harry Fenn. Photograph by Charles Klamkin.*)

of a more social character, and certainly, never before or since, was more hospitality dispensed by any occupant of the White House." Other sources say that she had her uncle's second wife act as official hostess in her stead and that she was seldom seen outside of the family quarters.

The truth is, perhaps, somewhere in between; and it is likely that Mrs. Pierce did enter the White House in retirement, since she was obviously in deep mourning at the time. She was also tubercular. In any case, there seems to be no report of the period that records the White House entertainments during the Pierce administration as having been any fun.

Jane Pierce, whose father was president of Bowdoin College, had been carefully educated, and she was a woman of quiet and refined taste. It does seem to be a matter of record that she hated politics and that she had tried her best to keep her husband from being involved, perhaps because of his "weakness."

57

When President Pierce moved into the White House, Congress appropriated $25,000 for improvements to the building. Pierce installed a furnace and used the money for other improvements. He also purchased china in 1855. The Pierce china has a deep pink border with gold banding and is French Limoges made by Haviland and Company. (See Fig. 12, Plate 14.)

In 1969, when workmen were excavating at the site of the White House swimming pool, two storage bins were uncovered that were thought to date from Thomas Jefferson's time. Other relics were dug up at the same time, among which was a dinner plate from the Haviland set made for President Pierce. The long burial had caused the deep pink rim to fade to a dusty rose. Mr. James Ketchum, curator at the White House during this period, said that it was the only Pierce dinner plate to come into the White House collection. However, a 1908 drawing disputes this statement. Mr. Ketchum also said that the plate, when mended, "will join the other exhibits of Presidential porcelain, glass and flatware collected in the 'China Room' on the ground floor of the executive mansion." However, three years later, the mended plate was not yet in evidence in its intended spot.

In the story of White House china, the Pierce administration is perhaps somewhat more interesting for what was not purchased than for what was. Indirectly, the Pierces were responsible for the china choices of President Buchanan and Mary Todd Lincoln. Two plates, displayed in the Crystal Palace Exhibition in New York in 1853, were offered as patterns designed for the President of the United States. Although the Pierces did not purchase either of these sets and opted for what was a much less elaborate and probably less expensive china pattern, both specimen plates were obviously more appealing to the next two occupants of the White House.

CHAPTER 16

James Buchanan
1857–1861

The White House took on a much gayer atmosphere during the administration of James Buchanan than it had seen in the past four administrations. This was not due to the fact that Buchanan, our only President to have remained a bachelor during his lifetime, was an especially outgoing man. The party atmosphere in the Executive Mansion came about through Buchanan's choice of official hostess, his niece and ward, Harriet Lane. Buchanan had assumed guardianship of four children when his sister and her husband died within two years of each other. Harriet, the youngest of the four, was Buchanan's favorite, and she lived with him during most of her childhood.

Blonde, attractive, and equipped with an education thought suitable for a lady in the mid-nineteenth century, Miss Lane accompanied her uncle to England during his ambassadorship to the Court of St. James. She became a great favorite of Queen Victoria and learned the ways of court life while in England. Interestingly, Laura C. Holloway, our nineteenth-century biographer, states, "And now she became publicly identified with Mr. Buchanan. At dinners and upon all occasions, she ranked, not as a niece, or even daughter, but as his wife." By the

59

time Harriet Lane assumed her duties as hostess of the White House, she was self-assured, poised, and already had a reputation for being a great beauty.

Harriet Lane, in contrast with the reluctant First Ladies who had preceded her, was everything that the country thought a First Lady should be. She was young, attractive, and did the "correct" thing. Just as she was a part of the reason for Buchanan's social and political success in England, so in large part did she make Buchanan's life in the White House pleasant and socially successful.

James Buchanan did not find his salary sufficient for the amount or quality of entertaining that he felt befitted a President of the United States, and he quite willingly subsidized the lavish parties given during his administration from his own pocket. Like Monroe, he had a great admiration for the French, and most particularly for French court entertaining. Therefore, Buchanan's entertainments were formal (some felt too formal), and the food served was French. His attractive and vivacious young hostess presided at all state affairs.

The greatest social coup of Buchanan's administration was a five day visit from the Prince of Wales to the White House in 1860. This was the first visit of an heir apparent to the British throne to the United States. It came about when Buchanan learned that the nineteen-year-old Prince would be visiting Canada. The handsome Prince, later to become Edward VII, traveled across the Canadian border to Washington; and no effort was spared to entertain the Prince in the royal manner. It is said that Buchanan even gave up his bedroom for His Royal Highness and slept on a cot near his office.

Two elaborate entertainments were planned for the Prince of Wales during the important visit. Washington was wild with excitement, and an invitation to either of the two formal dinners was a coveted piece of paper. Upon the Prince's return to England, Queen Victoria wrote to Buchanan, "He can not sufficiently praise the great cordiality with which he has been everywhere greeted in your country, and the friendly manner in which you have received him; and whilst, as a mother, I am grateful for the kindness shown him, I feel impelled to express at the same time, how deeply I have been touched by the many demonstrations of affection personally toward myself which his presence has called forth."

There has been much conjecture concerning the china used during the

Fig. 13 Engraving from *The New York Exhibition Illustrated* (1853), showing two plates designed and decorated for Presidential use in White House. These plates were originally designed for President Pierce, but he purchased the red-edged service instead. Haviland sold pattern on the right to Mary Todd Lincoln. Plate on the left was probably purchased by President Buchanan as part of dessert service. Plates were shown in Crystal Palace Exhibition in 1853 in New York. (*Photograph by Charles Klamkin.*)

Buchanan administration, since few objects survive which have heretofore been attributed to it. Probably one of the reasons for the lack of adequate records is that, as with other expenses attached to his lavish entertainment, Buchanan might have purchased some of the White House china with his own money. The record states that the Buchanan china was of French manufacture. One surviving plate is from a set purchased by Buchanan from a retiring French minister and has a deep purple-pink border outlined with bands of gold. A painted landscape is the center decoration. A white and gold teacup and saucer is another Buchanan china relic. This was purchased at one of the "decayed furniture sales" held after the Buchanan administration and eventually came into the hands of Mrs. Theodore Roosevelt. Another cup and saucer with typical Pennsylvania Dutch design is owned by a private collector and is attributed to the Buchanan estate.

For the most elaborate china pattern that can be traced no further back than the Buchanan era, however, one must look to the China Room at the White House. On display in that room is a large porcelain bowl, 25½ inches in height, that is supported by a pedestal of three bisque caryatids. The base is heavily gilded, and the decoration is blue and gold on white. This bowl has been given two different attributions in White House publications, the most recent being in a book called *The White House*, published by the White House Historical Association. It is called a "Rococo-Revival Punchbowl, with superb bisque caryatids, probably from the Jackson service." Displayed prominently under a glass cover, it is claimed to be the oldest piece of porcelain in continual use at the President's mansion. It has alternately been called a "punch bowl" and a "fruit bowl." Technically, it is neither. It is what was known in the mid-nineteenth century as a "centerpiece." (See Plate 15.)

Because of its size and the elaborate nature of its shape, this bowl figures frequently in literature written about the White House china collection. It is known to have been used in the White House during the Lincoln administration, but it was first written about during the Harrison administration. Mrs. Harrison found the bowl in a closet (some reports say in the attic, but others claim it was in the pantry) while she was organizing a collection of Presidential china for display in the White House. When found, the centerpiece was broken in three pieces, and Mrs. Harrison had it mended.

In 1903, A. G. Baker wrote an article for *Munsey's Magazine,* entitled "The China of the Presidents," in which she said that a Captain Pendel, the senior employee of the White House staff at the time, remembered seeing the bowl used during the Lincoln administration, "but it disappeared." Mrs. Baker further states that when Mrs. Harrison unearthed the bowl years afterward "in the garret broken in three pieces," she had it mended so deftly that the defect is almost imperceptible, "and it is now one of the display pieces in the family dining room." Mrs. Baker called it a "tall piece of unknown origin," and her article shows an illustration of the piece filled with white fern. Although Mrs. Harrison is credited with having had the glass case made to protect the piece, this would indicate that in 1903 the bowl was still being used.

An attempt to date the centerpiece has led to some interesting conjecture among the early writers on the subject of Presidential china. Alice Morse Earle, in her book *China Collecting in America,* described the china pattern of which the centerpiece is a part: "The Andrew Jackson set was of heavy and rather coarse bluish porcelain, apparently of Chinese manufacture, with bands of ugly blue and coarsely applied gold, and a conventional and clumsy shield in the centre. . . . it was not very tasteful nor beautiful, any more than was its Presidential owner, and very fitly furnished forth his dining-table." Obviously, Mrs. Earle allowed her political prejudices to interfere with her objectivity when it came to Presidential china. This kind of bias has not been at all unusual in Presidential china attributions.

Mrs. Earle does not say on what evidence she based her attribution of this china pattern to Andrew Jackson. However, since her book was written before 1892, it is probable that she acquired her knowledge from an article written in 1889 in the *Ladies' Home Journal* by Theodore Davis, the artist who designed the Hayes china.

Mr. Davis, obviously of the same political leanings as Mrs. Earle, said of the china pattern:

> The Jackson set was a departure. Although porcelain, it was remarkably heavy. Many of the pieces were specked with blemishes which would condemn them today to be sold to inexperienced purchasers. These pieces are all heavily banded with gilt a quarter of an inch in width, which band

> is burnished to the semblance of a polished metallic edge. Except cups and saucers, the edges of all the dishes and plates are of irregular shape.... A line of overglaze blue equal in length to the gilt which it joins completes the blue and gold border, within which is an inch wide gold band finished by delicate lines, first of blue, then of gold. The center is a conventional shield. The set would be called showy, but it is not one which would have been selected by a lady of the refined taste of Andrew Jackson's wife, who died shortly after her husband's election to the presidency. In fact, the set has been more than once designated by estimable women as "a man's set," whatever that may be.

It is somewhat amusing that Davis thought that Jackson's pipe-smoking Rachel would have had taste in china superior to her husband's. Andrew Jackson, as it happens, knew "good" when he saw it. (See Plate 15.)

An illustration in Mr. Davis's article proves beyond doubt that the three pieces shown—a dinner plate, a saucer, and a serving dish—are of the same pattern as the famous centerpiece now in the China Room. The one discrepancy in the Davis description of the service is the poor quality of the porcelain, itself. While the plates are heavy and not fine china, the centerpiece porcelain is of good quality and has no blemishes. However, this can easily be explained, and will be later on in this chapter.

Theodore Davis further states that he saw "pieces of this set on the table of the White House at the time of the Prince of Wales visit in 1860, upon which occasion the dishes were more or less odd, but generally comprised what is known as the red edge set, purchased during the administration of Franklin Pierce."

Abby Gunn Baker, a writer of many articles on the White House china collection and the one person most responsible for preserving what was left in the White House of Presidential china after the turn of the century, came up with a different identification of the centerpiece in an article written for *The Century Magazine* in 1908, entitled "The White House Collection of Presidential China." Mrs. Baker said, "Some years after [the discovery of the centerpiece by Mrs. Harrison] through William Crook, who has been on the clerical force of the executive office for more than 40 years, this piece was identified by the late Mrs. Nealy of Georgetown. She has a most interesting collection of colonial china of her own, and in searching some old Virginian records, she identified this bowl with the set of Madison china that was destroyed when the British burned the President's house in 1814."

Other writers of the early part of this century identified the centerpiece as dating from the Madison administration. Private collectors who own matching plates in the same pattern have also been satisfied to believe that the service was from the Madison era. The romance of having objects that escaped the ransacking and burning of the White House gives the service more interesting provenance. The service, or the few remaining pieces of it, has alternately been called "French" or "Chinese."

A description of a cup and saucer from this same service in a 1954 Parke-Bernet sale (April 30 and May 1) of *Select Early American Furniture and Silver, American Historical China, Paintings, Glass and other Property From the Collection of Stanley S. Wohl, Annapolis, Maryland, and from other owners* is given as "No. 277. James Madison (1809–1917) Porcelain Breakfast Cup and Saucer. Valenced blue and gold edge enclosing a banding of scattered gilded pellets centring a cartouche, with interior with a deep gilded band. *Vieux Paris* (Wohl)." A note in the catalogue calls the cup and saucer "unique, and probably the only existing example in private hands." It also informs the auction goers, "This historic cup and saucer, in addition to a plate and teacup and saucer (now in the China Room of the White House) and the Stuart portrait of Washington in the East Room, are believed to be the only furnishings of the White House to survive the burning by the British in 1814."

It is surprising that no mention is made in the Parke-Bernet catalogue of the large centerpiece, obviously a part of the same service. It was on display in the China Room at the time and was also attributed to Madison on the identification card that then accompanied it.

Ada Walker Camehl, in *The Blue-China Book*, which is the most recent book published to have any mention of Presidential china (with the exception of White House publications) also attributes this same porcelain service to the Madison administration. Quoting William Lee, who was in charge of refurbishing the burned White House before Monroe moved in, Mrs. Camehl writes that " 'there was no recourse in the remnants of glass, earthenware, china, linen, etc., of which scarcely an article would serve; indeed, we may say, there remained none of these articles fit for use.'" Nevertheless, Mrs. Camehl was able to justify the attribution of the service to Madison by stating that

> a number of pieces of a beautiful set of French porcelain now known as the "Dolly [sic] Madison china" are claimed to have escaped the catastrophe, and two examples of it—a plate and a tea cup and saucer—are preserved in the collection of presidential ware. Another piece of the same set, which Mrs. Harrison after she became mistress of the Mansion found broken in three parts upon the White House pantry shelves and which she had carefully put together, is an exquisite punch-bowl about two feet in height, the bowl upheld by figures of the three Graces resting upon a standard.

It is only natural that one should begin to suspect White House attributions of china when even the location of the centerpiece's discovery is given by three different sources as "the garret," "a closet," "the pantry."

Mrs. Camehl also tells us that at the time of her writing, the "punch bowl" adorned a small table in the private White House dining room. She describes the decoration of the bowl as being dainty and of blue and gold, its distinguishing characteristics being the wide bands filled with small gold dots and bordered with fine blue and gold lines, which encircle the specimen, together with the blue and gold shield-shaped decoration filled with dots that marks the centers of the flat pieces. Although this writer was not prejudiced by earlier descriptions of the service, she was certainly influenced by earlier writers' claims that the china had belonged to James and Dolley Madison.

It is no wonder that the White House identification card on the centerpiece has changed from time to time, giving both Dolley Madison and Andrew Jackson a chance at ownership. However, in order to make a more accurate identification of the controversial service, it is necessary to consider more than the political history of the nineteenth century. Some knowledge of the state of the art of ceramics would have been even more helpful to the earlier writers and to those responsible for cataloguing the China Room objects. The service of which the centerpiece is a part is not Chinese but French. It is of a type of porcelain that was produced in France after 1840, and in truth, it is heavier than many other examples of French porcelain made during the nineteenth century. The clay body is a type that was produced at Limoges to compete with the British Queen's ware and other earthenware products of the Staffordshire potteries that were in general use in America at the time. The fashion for whiteware and the discovery of kaolin (white clay) in the Limoges district of France in the eighteenth century had made it possible for whiteware to be produced, but this ware could not compete in price with the British creamware. It was not until the mid-nineteenth century that a heavier, coarser porcelain could be produced that was competitive in price with British products but was white in color. This ware was very much like the Canton china that was so much in favor in the United States.

The "irregular shape" of the plates as described by Mr. Davis was not an unusual shape for the mid-nineteenth century. As a matter of fact, the shape was almost identical to the Lincoln china, purchased later. The "Rococo Revival" design of the centerpiece is typical not of Madison or Jackson's era, but of the middle of the nineteenth century, Buchanan's time. The unglazed biscuit figures, which form the stem of the centerpiece, are of a type of porcelain that was extremely popular during the 1850's. The British, the French, and even the American potters (at Bennington, Vermont) were all manufacturing statuettes in what was called "Parian" ware. The decorative blue and gold border of the service, hardly Chinese, is a lambrequin pattern, a design that became extremely popular in the decorative arts of the mid-nineteenth century. The center shield, although probably inspired by earlier Chinese plate decoration, is also an adaptation of the lambrequin shape.

The discrepancy in the quality of the body of the useful plates as opposed to the decorative centerpiece can easily be explained when one is aware of the potter's problems in firing such a large ceramic object. It is highly probable that the kilns at Limoges could not accommodate a piece of such elaborate design and size. The centerpiece was probably made at Sèvres, although it was apparently decorated with the remainder of the service.

Because of the above conjecture and evidence, further proof is necessary to place this important relic in its proper place in history. Exhibitions of art and industry were an important method of advertising and promotion for nineteenth-century manufacturers. The Exhibition of 1853, held in the specially constructed Crystal Palace in New York, caused European as well as American manufacturers to display elaborate and showy merchandise. At this display, Minton, a British potter, showed an elaborate centerpiece very similar in style to the White House centerpiece.

On the theory that such an ambitious ceramic effort as the White House centerpiece would, had it been made by that time, have been a part of a French

Fig. 14 Plate and custard cup attributed to President James Buchanan. (*The Smithsonian Institution. Photograph by Charles Klamkin.*)

potter's display at the exhibition, catalogues were searched. Scholarship being its own reward, the *New York Exhibition Illustrated*, published at the time of the Crystal Palace Exhibition, turned out to contain an illustration and explanation, not of the centerpiece, but of a plate that matches it.

The firm of E. V. Haughwout and Company of New York, china merchants, displayed two china patterns that were later illustrated in the exhibition publication. Both china patterns, manufactured by Haviland in Limoges, France, were presented for consideration to President Pierce; and one of the patterns, with modifications, was later ordered by Mrs. Lincoln. The second plate, with the exception of an initial in the shield, is identical to the plates that match the centerpiece. The catalogue describes the engravings as "Two plates, with the cipher of the President and the arms of the United States form part of a series for the use of that functionary."

President Pierce turned down these Haviland designs in favor of the red-edged service. It is probable that the blue and gold china was later purchased by Buchanan to augment what was left of the Pierce china. Most likely, the blue and gold service was simply a dessert service, since the only remaining pieces seem to be of the sizes and shapes that were then included in dessert services. It is probable that if Pierce did order this service, he would have had it made with his initial, as shown in the engraving. (See Fig. 14.)

In any case, the famous centerpiece cannot be attributed to any administration before 1853, the earliest possible date that Haviland would have produced the set. The earliest recollection of the centerpiece in use at the White House is Davis's, who saw it on the table at the dinner given for the Prince of Wales in 1860. Therefore, it is a safe assumption that Buchanan did purchase this service. It is possible, of course, that further evidence may come to light that places the service in Pierce's administration, but it would have been uncharacteristic of Jane Pierce or her husband to have ordered such an elaborate set. One would prefer to think of it as having been the choice of the popular and pretty Harriet Lane and her indulgent uncle, James Buchanan.

CHAPTER 17

Abraham Lincoln
1861–1865

Whatever else has been said about Mary Todd Lincoln, few can deny that history has shown that she was probably the most compulsive shopper among our First Ladies. As soon as Mrs. Lincoln had been given the $20,000 Congress appropriated for furnishings for the White House, she set out on a shopping trip to New York. China for the White House was badly needed by that time. The obvious place to look for White House china would have been E. V. Haughwout and Company. This firm had imported and decorated the china of the past two administrations.

As luck would have it, Haughwout still had one china pattern left from the Crystal Palace Exhibition in 1853 that was specially designed for the President's mansion. The Haughwout salesman obviously had little trouble in convincing Mrs. Lincoln that this was the service she should order. However, whereas the original service exhibited was blue-bordered, Mrs. Lincoln chose a purple-red border. Another modification seems to have been in the shape of the plates, which in the original engraving are only slightly scalloped. The Lincoln plates are more closely the same pronounced shape as the Buchanan plates. It is not known whether this change was made because Haviland had a supply of the whiteware in this shape available for decorating or because Mrs. Lincoln preferred the more elaborate shape. It is probable that the former was the reason, since delivery on the entire order took only four and a half months. The order was probably given in the middle of May, 1861, when Mrs. Lincoln was reported by the newspapers as having gone shopping in New York; and the entire service—190 pieces in the dinner service, a matching 208-piece dessert service in the same pattern, and a 260-piece breakfast and tea service—was delivered on September 2 of the same year. Of interest to those who followed the story of the White House centerpiece in chapter 16 is the listing in the bill of "Two Large Centre Pieces, Sèvres, supported by White Pelicans and decorated to match dinner service." These pieces were sold to Mrs. Lincoln for $100 apiece. If still in existence, it is probable that they would be very close in size and design to the Buchanan centerpiece. The "Pelicans" were undoubtedly a substitute for the caryatids in the earlier display piece, and it is a safe bet that they, too, were Parian. "Two punch bowls" are also listed, proving once and for all that a

Fig. 15 Drawing of punch bowl from Lincoln state dinner service. Note that gold line decoration is similar in style to Buchanan dessert service. (*From The Century Magazine, October, 1908. Drawing by Harry Fenn. Photograph by Charles Klamkin.*)

centerpiece is not a punch bowl. Nor was it technically a fruit bowl, since "Eight High Comportiers for fruit" were included in the order. However, these were not to be made at Sèvres but were a part of the plates produced by Haviland at Limoges. The rapid delivery of this large lot of china would lead one to assume that Haughwout had the whiteware for most of the three services in stock. A total of 658 pieces was delivered, all decorated in the same pattern, with a gold rope border, a solferino inner border, and the American eagle and part of the shield on a cloud in the center. (See Figs. 15, 16, Plate 16.)

The Lincoln china is of a quality similar to the Haviland blue and gold ordered by the previous administration. The complaints of the White House kitchen help may explain why so little is left of the previous dessert service, which undoubtedly was not purchased in any great amount to begin with. The Lincoln china is said to have broken too easily, not from neglect when being handled, but because of the quality of the china itself. However, Mrs. Lincoln liked the service well enough to order a set for herself with the initials, "M.L." in place of the arms of the United States. During Lincoln's campaign for re-election, the editor of the New York *World* accused the Lincolns of padding the original bill

Fig. 16 Double-handled custard cup from Lincoln state china. *(The Smithsonian Institution)*

for the state china to include their personal service. However, a bill exists to prove this accusation untrue.

Soon after Lincoln's re-election, Mary Lincoln ordered another service for the tables of the White House. Hardly a shopper to be bullied by campaign accusations, Mrs. Lincoln purchased a set of buff-bordered china, in quieter taste than the first service. It, too, is of French manufacture and was ordered from J. K. Kerr of Philadelphia. The President was assassinated two months after the delivery of this service, and the bill for it was not paid by the government until a year later.

Another china service with Lincoln provenance is a Royal Worcester service that was used at the Soldier's Home, the summer White House. This service, or the few remaining pieces of it, is decorated with a wide border of yellow and gray flowers in a diaper pattern and with a wreath of flowers in the center. It was undoubtedly a stock pattern and is interesting because it was the earliest recorded purchase of English china for the White House that has been noted.

The Haviland china would not have given Mary Todd Lincoln a great deal of pleasure, save when it was new. By the time she left the White House, the inventory listed "3 small remnants of china sets nearly all broken up." The "one full set of china" listed was undoubtedly the buff-bordered service. The early Haviland china was white. It simply was not very strong.

Although the Smithsonian Institution's only publication on Presidential china, *White House China of the Lincoln Administration*, gives the information that "the original pieces of the Lincoln service did not bear any mark on the reverse," this does not seem to be fact. In the exhibit called "Dinner with the Presidents" held at the Chicago Art Institute between October 27 and December 3, 1961, four plates from the Lincoln service were loaned from the White House. Of these four, Hans Huth, then Curator of Decorative Arts, listed two (a 9½ inch dinner plate and a 7⅝ inch salad plate) as being marked by Haviland and Company, Limoges, France. Haviland did not mark every piece in their sets of china at that time, but it is obvious that at least some of the plates had marks. These might have been from the Johnson reorder, but there is no way to prove this since the White House certainly did not keep the original service and the Johnson plates separate. There seems, therefore, to be little doubt that the Smithsonian publication is in error on this point. (See Plates 16, 17.)

CHAPTER 18

Andrew Johnson
1865–1869

The White House was again in a sorry state when the Andrew Johnsons moved into it. Lincoln had allowed free access to the building during the Civil War, and soldiers had camped out in the downstairs rooms. The furniture was ruined and filthy. The weeks after the assassination that Mary Todd Lincoln spent pulling herself together before she could or would vacate the White House had taken their toll, also. Nothing was cared for during that period.

Whereas Mary Lincoln's early social life in the White House had been flamboyant, Eliza Johnson was an invalid and took no part in Washington's social life. A contemporary report of a Washington correspondent said "Mrs. Johnson, a confirmed invalid, has never appeared in Washington society. Her very existence is a myth to almost everyone."

The Johnsons' daughter, Martha Patterson, assumed the role of White House hostess. More than that, Mrs. Patterson once again made the White House habitable with a $30,000 congressional appropriation. The eldest of the Johnsons' five children, she had been used to taking charge. She managed to stretch the money allowed her for redoing the White House by re-covering old furniture and freshening the state rooms with new wallpaper.

Martha Patterson presided over many elegant state dinners, and the large dining room, which had been closed for the last few years of the Lincoln administration, was refurbished as far as the budget would allow.

The State Dining Room was described by a friend of the Johnsons upon a visit to the Presidential mansion:

> Late in the afternoon I was sitting in the cheerful room occupied by the invalid mother when Mrs. Patterson came for me to go and see the table. The last State dinner was to be given this night, and the preparations for the occurence had been commensurate with those former occasions. I looked at the invalid [Mrs. Johnson], whose feet had never crossed the apartment to which we were going, and by whom the elegant entertainments over which her daughter presided, were totally unenjoyed. Through the hall and down the stairway, I followed my hostess and stood beside her in the grand old room. It was a beautiful and altogether rare scene which I viewed in the quiet light of this closing winter day, and the recollections and associations of the time linger most vividly in memory now. The table was arranged for forty persons, each guest's name being upon the plate designated in the invitation list.
>
> In the center stood three magnificent ormolu ornaments filled with fadeless flowers, while beside each plate was a bouquet of odorous greenhouse exotics. It was not the color or design of the Sèvres china of green and gold, the fragile glass, nor yet the massive plate which attracted my admiration, but the harmony of the whole, which satisfied and refreshed.

The Johnsons evidently liked the Lincoln state china and ordered pieces to fill in the set when they had been in the White House a while. There were few of the original pieces left, and the Johnson order placed with E. V. Haughwout was a substantial one. A voucher in the National Archives shows that the charges for the porcelain were $2,061.25.

The Lincoln buff-edged service was new at the start of the Johnson administration, but obviously this did not last, either. The "Sèvres china of green and gold" mentioned above as having been used on the table for the last state dinner given by the Johnsons is probably the china representing that administration in the china collection at the White House. In an article written by J. K. Thomson for *Antiques Journal,* July, 1961, this china is described as "American-made 'Lyons' (green ribbon and floral design, with a green landscape inset)."

The Staffordshire plate illustrated on Plate 17 is said to have belonged to the Johnsons. It is a pattern that was in general distribution at the time and was probably a family piece. Of the "Sèvres china of green and gold" described by the Johnsons' friend, nothing definite seems to be known.

CHAPTER 19

Ulysses Simpson Grant
1869–1877

Frequently the White House occupants with the least-pretentious beginnings are responsible for the most opulent administrations. Such was the case when Ulysses S. Grant and his First Lady, Julia Dent Grant, entered the White House in 1869. From plain Ohio beginnings, the war hero found himself with undreamed-of power in an affluent postwar economy. Four children, three sons and the popular daughter, Nellie Grant, as well as Mrs. Grant's father, became the occupants of 1600 Pennsylvania Avenue.

Mrs. Grant, who seemed to be somewhat insecure concerning her ability to act as hostess in the mansion, went to enormous expense and effort to see that the White House entertainments were the cause of conversation throughout the country. The army chef that her husband had brought to the White House was dismissed, and an Italian steward, Melah, replaced him. Elaborate meals with as many as thirty courses were served on a horseshoe-shaped table in the State Dining Room.

Expense did not seem to matter during the Grant administration. Dinner went on for hours, leaving little time afterward for conversation or entertainment. The usual after-dinner period of sociability was cut to fifteen or twenty minutes after most large dinners. (See Fig. 17.)

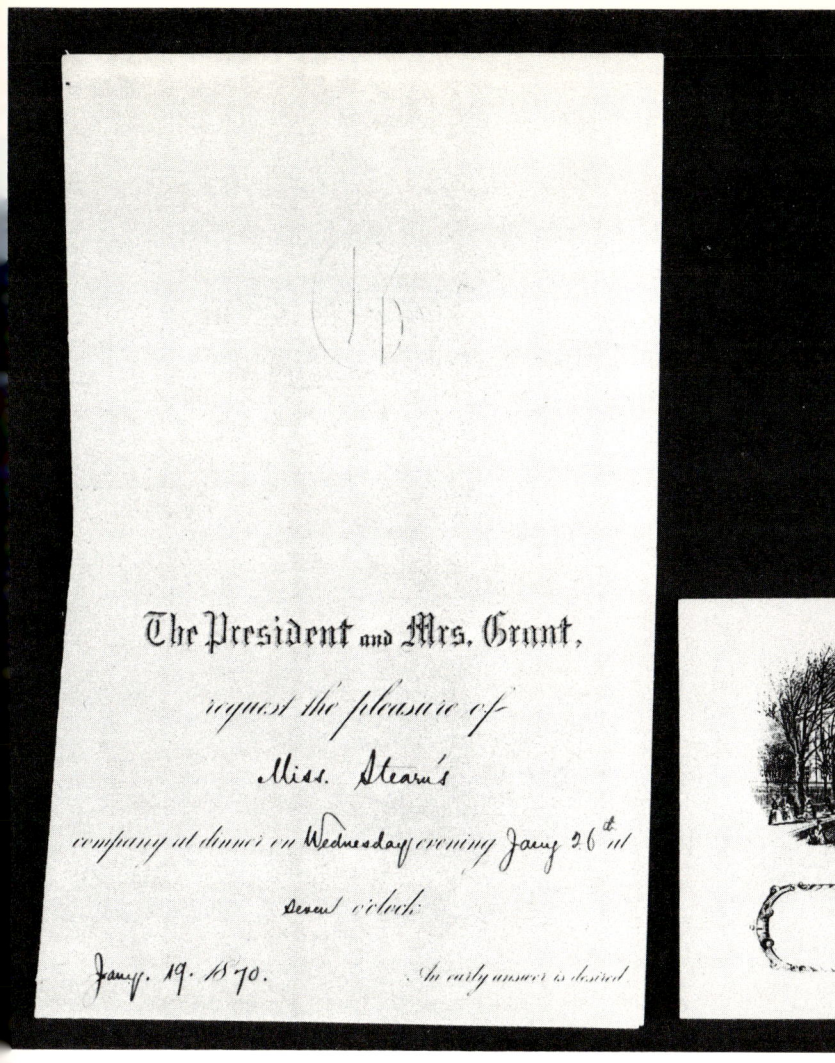

ig. 17   Dinner invitation sent by President and Mrs. Grant from the White House. (*The Smithsonian Institution*)

Not only were the formal meals gargantuan and extravagant but the family dinners almost always included extra guests. It is said that six extra settings were routinely placed in the family dining room. Mrs. Grant, in addition, held a reception one afternoon a week. These receptions were open to the public, admission simply requiring that a calling card be left at the front door.

The Grant entertainments were routinely reported in the daily papers and seldom was Mrs. Grant's hospitality criticized in any way. The public seemed to enjoy a vicarious interest in the reports of "sumptuous banquets" and "brilliant affairs." It was only at the end of Grant's eight years in the White House that he realized the financial burden this entertainment had been.

In order to accommodate the grand style of entertaining of the Grants, the

White House was renovated and cleaned during the summer of 1869 while the Grants vacationed at Long Branch. It is probable that the Grant china was ordered at the very beginning of the administration, since it was delivered on February 10, 1870. Archive records show that Grant state service to have cost $3,000. The service was ordered from the importers and dealers J. W. Boteler and Brother, 320 Pennsylvania Avenue, Washington, D.C. (See Figs. 18, 20.)

Fig. 18 Mark found on some pieces of the Grant china. Haviland has reproduced Presidential plates several times in the past. (*Private collection. Photograph by Charles Klamkin.*)

The Grant dinner service is described in the Boteler bill as "buff, with flowers and coat of arms." The shape of the plates is the irregular scallop-edged design of the Lincoln and Buchanan plates. The flowers are in the center of the plates, and the small coat of arms is placed in the border. The outside edge is rimmed in gold. (See Fig. 19.)

The floral decorations, all different and all American, were originally drawn by an American artist, William E. Seaton. These drawings were then sent to Limoges, where they were adapted for china decoration by Lissac, painter-engraver of the Haviland and Company decorating department. Lissac, who was head of his department at the time, was also one of the artists to work on the Hayes china at a later date. A different flower appears on each of the Grant plates, and all the flowers are indigenous to America.

The new Grant china did not arrive in time for the state dinner the President and Mrs. Grant held on January 26, 1870, for Queen Victoria's son, Prince Arthur. The dinner service was not delivered until the following month. It is

Fig. 19 Dinner plate from state china service of the Ulysses S. Grant administration. Made by Haviland. (*The Smithsonian Institution*)

probable that for this occasion the Grants used a dinner service that had belonged to Edwin M. Stanton, Lincoln's Secretary of War, whom Grant had replaced in that position in the Johnson administration. It is said that this service was given to the White House after Lincoln's death and was used along with remnants of the Lincoln china until the delivery of the Grant service. These plates have a rose du Barry border and are initialed "E.M.S." (See Plates 17, 18.)

Fig. 20 Mark found on Grant state china soup bowl with decoration of wild rose. Haviland did not consistently mark all china at this time. *(The Smithsonian Institution)*

Unquestionably, the most elaborate of all the Grant entertainments given at the White House was the wedding of President Grant's only daughter, Nellie, to Algernon Charles Frederick Sartoris in May, 1874. Nellie had met Mr. Sartoris on the ship on which she had returned from a socially triumphant tour of Europe. Although her father disapproved of the marriage, he and Mrs. Grant still went all out to prepare for the first White House wedding to be held in thirty years.

Additional china (299 pieces costing $1,411) in the Grant pattern was ordered for the occasion, which at the time was called "the finest wedding ever known in Washington." Two hundred guests were present, and they represented the officials of government and their families; the Army, Navy, and Marine Corps and their families; the diplomatic corps; and personal friends of the Grants. Floral decorations for the wedding were described as being "superb, those of the East Room [where the wedding was held] being the finest." White satin menus and favors of small boxes of wedding cake tied with satin ribbons were taken home by the guests.

The Grant style of entertaining was described by Mrs. Holloway, who lived through the eight years of the administration:

The eight years social administration of Mrs. Grant was characterized by great elegance and dignity. All official and social observances were conducted on a scale of magnificence, and the mansion, itself, richly furnished. Costly plate and decorations were supplied and the entertainments were on a more elaborate scale than had marked previous administrations.

The official entertainments were frequent, and the social career of Mrs. Grant as Lady of the White House closed with one of the most brilliant receptions ever given in the White House.

The White House under Mrs. Grant's social administration was a delightful home, and was ever the abode of many relatives and friends who shared in the many pleasures it afforded. An atmosphere of pleasant social life was felt by all visitors at the executive mansion, and though Mrs. Grant was not particularly fond of society, her stay in the White House is remembered as a period of great gayety in Washington.

This was a report that must have warmed the heart of Julia Dent Grant. With these accolades to her virtues as hostess and First Lady of the land, what matter that Ulysses S. Grant, on his death bed, found it necessary to write his memoirs as a means of assuring an estate for his family?

CHAPTER 20

Rutherford Birchard Hayes
1877–1881

No china service previously ordered for the White House ever elicited so much publicity as the Haviland service designed and made for the Hayes administration. Certainly no previous Presidential plates are more typical of the decorative art style of the period in which they were made or represent so perfectly the interests of the First Lady who ordered them.

It was only natural that Lucy Webb Hayes, a trained botanist and lover of nature, should have ordered china that represented the flora and fauna of the United States. Mrs. Hayes entertained at the White House by giving elaborate dinners and receptions at which no alcohol was served. She was a product of the state of Ohio, the birthplace of the women's crusade against intemperance.

Lucy Hayes served an adequate apprenticeship for her role as First Lady when her husband became the congressman from Ohio and later governor of that state. An educated and religious woman, Mrs. Hayes was well liked by the press and was considered to be a brilliant hostess. Of her, Mrs. Holloway said, "Mrs. Hayes was delighted with the high place she had attained. She made no denial on this point, and freely admitted the satisfaction it gave her, and the enjoyment she hoped to have." Despite the lack of liquor in the White House menus, Lucy

Hayes was a popular Washington hostess who entertained in the high Victorian style of the period. Her first Saturday afternoon reception at the White House was held only four weeks after the inauguration. Mrs. Hayes was described by a guest who attended as having "eyes that looked as black as night, and they had a lustre rarely seen. Her whole face was positively radiant."

The second occasion for grand-scale entertainment at the Executive Mansion was a visit from the Russian Grand Dukes Alexis and Constantine. The gathering was described as

> brilliant as any ever assembled in the Executive Mansion. The drawing-rooms were elaborately decorated with flowers, and the State dining-room never presented a finer appearance. The table was a mass of flowers and cut-glass and Sèvres china. [White House china was frequently called "Sèvres."] In the center was an oval mirror representing a lake with tropical banks of ferns and trailing vines. In the center of the lake was an island of pink azaleas with cloth of gold roses, while over the outer surfaces were vines massed to look like water-lilies. The banks of the lake were strewn with graceful hills, formed with vases of tropical fruit, and here and there a pyramid or column of candied fruits and bon-bons rose between. At each end of the lake were tall frosted cakes decorated with white azaleas and pink and tea roses and smilax. Delicate pink and white vases of frosted glass and silver stands stood at each plate, the pink vases holding clusters of white buds and the white vases pink buds. Azalea trees, camellias and other flowering plants were arranged about the room, ornamenting by their proximity to them the chocolate and strawberry pyramids that stood at the north side of the room. Vines of smilax strung on gilt wires were draped about the table, chandeliers and pictures.

An exception to the "no wine with dinner" rule was taken on this occasion when the Secretary of State, Mr. Evarts, insisted that the guests of honor would miss wine since they were accustomed to having it with their meals. A great issue was made of this in the press, which was later informed that after the Russian dinner, no American citizen would be served wine while dining at the Executive Mansion. Lemonade Lucy also forbade cardplaying and other forms of gambling in the mansion.

Another outstanding entertainment of the Hayes administration took place on December 31, 1877, when the Hayeses celebrated a dry twenty-fifth wedding anniversary with an elaborate dinner party. The supper room was again described as "Magnificent with the most elegant table-ware in the Executive Mansion." It is not known what this "table-ware" was, since the Hayes china was not delivered until 1880. Most likely it was the Grant set of Haviland china.

The Hayes state china was the brain child of the American artist, Theodore R. Davis. Mrs. Hayes had already ordered a dinner service from Haviland that was to have had fern decoration. The contract had already been signed. Davis, an artist-reporter for *Harper's Weekly*, convinced Lucy Hayes that plates for the White House should be decorated by an American with American motifs. It was decided that American flowers, animals, and birds should be used; and the contract for the fern pattern was canceled. Davis was commissioned to execute the designs for the new plates. (See Plates 3, 18–20.)

Upon obtaining a release from his obligations to *Harper's*, Theodore Davis opened a studio in Asbury Park, New Jersey, where he painted 130 different water-color designs that included special motifs for fish, meat, game, and ice cream platters. He also modeled twelve new shapes for special plates to be used for various courses. One of the departures from the assortment of nature subjects was a dessert plate that showed a view of Davis's studio.

The story of the Hayes china is best told in an illustrated book issued by Haviland and Company, New York, in 1880. Titled *The White House Porcelain Service*, and subtitled *Designs by an American Artist Illustrating Exclusively American Fauna and Flora*, the book was a successful attempt to raise interest among china collectors in purchasing reproductions of the Hayes dinner service made to augment Haviland's losses in producing the elaborate set. This arrangement was made with President and Mrs. Hayes when Haviland honored the price quoted for the fern-decorated china and produced the more elaborate plates at the same price.

The Haviland book describes fully the history of the Hayes porcelain and its design and execution:

> The existence of kaoline, of superior quality, and in inexhaustible quantities, taken in connection with other advantages, induced David Haviland, an American merchant and founder of the house of Haviland & Co., to locate its potteries in Limoges, France.

At the Centennial Exhibition, Haviland & Co. made the most notable display of Porcelain and Faience, and later, at the Paris Exposition, received the Gold Medal and Cross of the Legion of Honor.

In the spring of 1879, an order was given to Haviland & Co. to furnish the Executive Mansion at Washington with a dinner service, which, as it was to be used only for state occasions, the President's wife desired would combine elegance and appropriate American decoration. The time specified for the completion of the set was limited, and the obstacles to be overcome unprecedented, and its successful production would involve innumerable trials of color; added to this, no European artist was known who was conversant with a wide range of American subjects and their appropriate use for the decoration of porcelain.

Mr. Theodore Haviland requested the aid of his friend Theodore R. Davis, who undertook the invention of shapes and the production of water-color studies, which Haviland & Co. have reproduced in china.

Mr. Davis possessed the artistic skill, and a knowledge as essential as it was remarkable. Professional duty, and a love of adventure, had led him to study the native flora and fauna in every part of the country. He had fished the rivers of the East and West and in the sea, hunted fowl and wild game in the forests, the swamps and the mountains; shot the buffalo on the plains, and visited the historic haunts of the Indians in the East; met the Indians in their wigwams, and studied their habits on the prairies of the far West.

The artist selected a unique atelier. The novelty of the studio induced Haviland & Co. to request him to furnish a water-color drawing of the place, which we introduce with the fruit series, where it is quite fully described. The location was chosen because of its convenience to subjects both from the sea, field and forest, and its location prevented the intrusion of visitors.

In presenting the service to the public, we desire to make some statements which seem to be important to enable a just criticism of it. The designs were made in water-color, and although in nearly every instance they were bold and striking, they were difficult to reproduce perfectly upon porcelain, with hard mineral color. And to successfully accomplish this, it was necessary to invent new methods, and to have recourse to peculiar mechanical appliances.

We coincided with the artist in the opinion that a high degree of finish should not be attempted in every plate, fearing the sacrifice of breadth and tone which he deemed necessary to the general effect of the series, when arranged upon the table. This was undoubtedly correct, for some of the plates, when examined singly, lose a part of their attractiveness, but the same plates, when placed upon the table, will not seem inferior to others, which may have been separately examined to more advantage. Another result thus obtained is the absence of the feeling of timidity noticeable in most examples of fine porcelain, where a high degree of finish is the principle feature of the decoration. It must not be inferred that we believe that coarse, inartistic drawing and design could ever compete with refined work, but we do insist that a plate, when decorated with a strong, firm drawing, closely studied from nature, which tells clearly the story of the subject, will attract more attention and be productive of more enjoyment than the plate which has great beauty of finish, but lacks the qualities noted above.

The Haviland book then goes on to list the artists who were involved in producing this unique porcelain service:

Theodore R. Davis	New York	Designer
Bracquemond	Auteuil	Etcher
Tochum	Auteuil	Chromiste
Valentine	Paris	Engraver
Lissac	Limoges	Painter
Chadal	Limoges	Manufacturer
Gourmault	Paris	Modeler
Valette	Limoges	Modeler
Charles Riroch	Limoges	Decorator
Lambert	Sèvres	Painter
Barbarin	Limoges	Painter
Laforest	Limoges	Painter
Hayon	Limoges	Painter
Duclair	Limoges	Painter
Dominique	Limoges	Painter
Mlle. Anna Daraud	Limoges	Gilder

The method by which the plates were decorated was new at the time. The lithography process of transferring designs to china was developed by Haviland at Limoges shortly before 1875. Using this process, it was possible to lay a pattern in several colors directly on the whiteware before glazing. The pattern on the stone was picked up on waxed paper and the paper laid on the plate. When the plate was refired in the kiln, the paint was struck into the glaze. This new method was used on the Hayes plates in addition to the more conventional copperplate engraving that had been developed in England after the middle of the eighteenth century. The diversity of designs for the Hayes china necessitated a diversity of methods in adapting the Davis water colors for porcelain decoration.

The composition of the Hayes service was also listed in the Haviland book. This information was followed by sketches of each design and the artist's notes or descriptions of his paintings and shapes. The remainder of the book includes a letter written to Mr. Haviland by Davis on completion of the designs and a short note from Mrs. Hayes sent to Theodore Davis upon delivery of the service by Haviland. The letter is dated August 2, 1880.

Each piece of the Hayes porcelain was signed and dated. The Great Seal of the United States was also placed on the undersides of the plates. The service consisted of more than 1,000 pieces, the largest White House service made to that date. The amount Haviland billed the government was around $4,000, an enormous bargain at $4 a plate. The dinner service probably cost Haviland and Company at least five times the billed price, and at the end of the Hayes administration, the firm attempted to cover some of their loss by producing pieces of the service for general sale to the public. These are dated "1881" on the obverse sides.

The Hayes china, although made and decorated in France, was in every way American in style. It started a vogue for all-over simulated hand-painted china with scenic designs that found a unique market in this country. Theodore Haviland was obviously well aware of the influence that White House china, properly promoted, could have on American taste; and he instructed his French pottery to produce like plates in quantity, decorated with all-over patterns.

High Victorian taste of the late nineteenth century demanded that as much decoration as possible be crammed onto the article being decorated. The desire for naturalistic forms and shapes was answered to the fullest in the Davis models. The Hayes plates were seldom used for the purpose for which they were designed after the original owners vacated the White House. High fashion seldom lasts long.

In 1903, however, writers were still extolling the beauty of the Hayes service. In an article in *Munsey's Magazine* in that year, Abby Gunn Baker wrote, "The

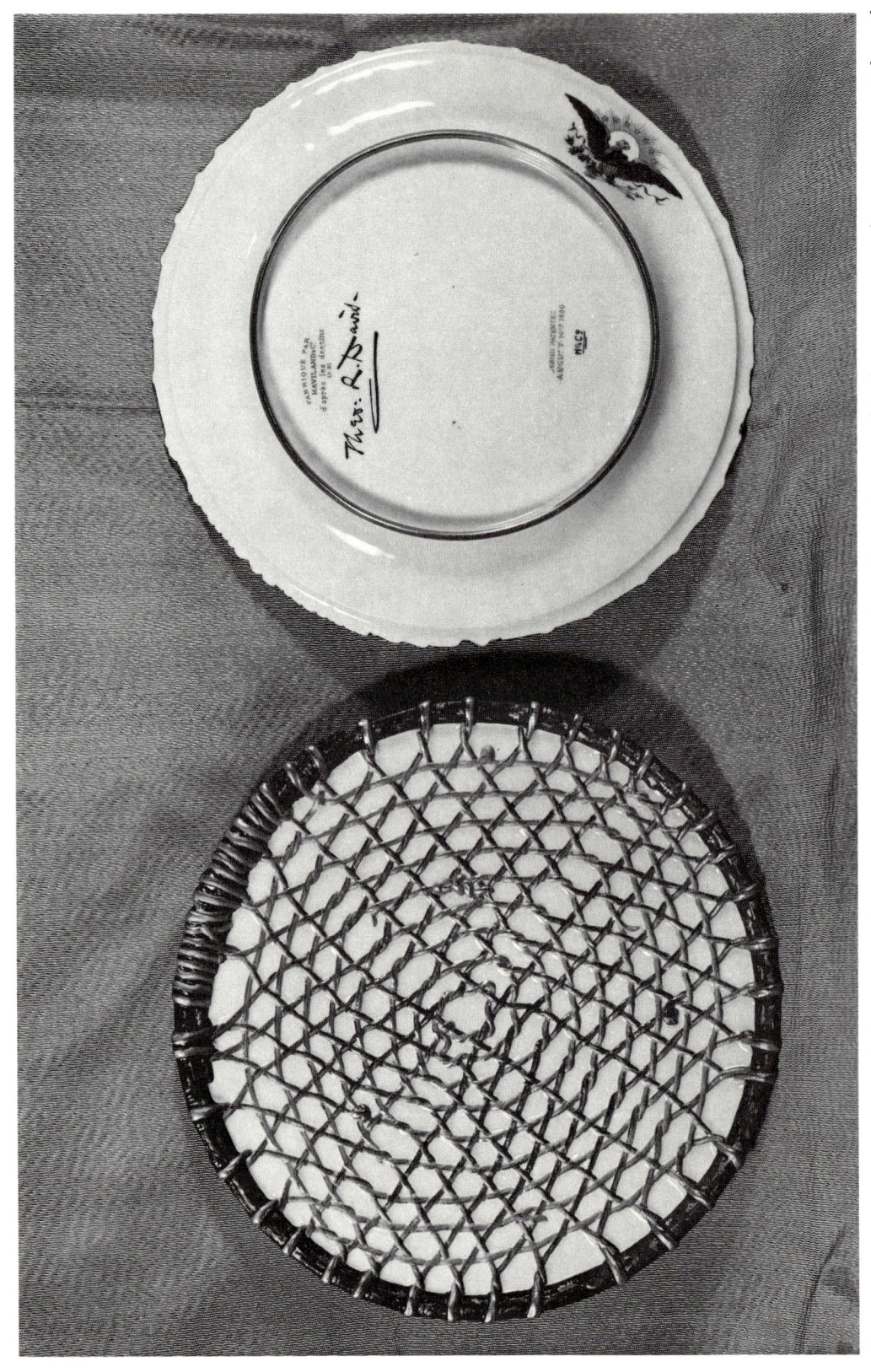

Fig. 21 Obverse and reverse of Hayes state china ice cream plate with "Snowshoe" design. Serving plate has entire snowshoe as pattern embossed and painted on it. (*The Smithsonian Institution*)

elaborately decorated Hayes set, designed by Theodore Davis, was undoubtedly one of the most beautiful ever made for the American market, but its reproduction in cheaper china ruined its value as Presidential ware. A greater quantity of it is still in use at the Executive Mansion than of any other set." (See Fig. 21.)

By 1908, the same writer complained that had the set been properly protected and not reproduced, as was also the Harrison design, it would have been far more valuable. By 1922, Mrs. Baker seemed to have gained some perspective about the Hayes service. She wrote, "The decoration is of the highly naturalistic style which was popular at the time of the Hayes Administration, and while often criticized by connoisseurs yet the dishes are an unfailing source of conversation at White House dinners."

Although later Presidents displayed the Hayes porcelain, few of them used it for table settings, and many pieces of the service were sold at the various auctions of decayed furnishings from the White House.

Mrs. Lyndon Johnson, in her book *A White House Diary*, mentions the Hayes china as being used during a luncheon for a group interested in historic preservation. She calls the service "incredible," which, of course, it is. She also mentions using the Hayes "funny china dishes" for ash trays in the White House. Perhaps the most reasonable explanation of why the Hayes dinner service became unpopular so quickly was given recently when an expert in the history of porcelain asked, "Who wants to see the animal you've just finished eating in its natural habitat?"

CHAPTER 21

James Abram Garfield
1881

President and Mrs. Hayes had a feeling for historical objects and during the Hayes administration had spent several weeks each summer at Speigel Grove, Fremont, Ohio, to which they brought various White House articles that they thought should be saved for history. This was the first acknowledgment by any President and his wife that not only the federal Union but the historical artifacts that represented its history should be preserved.

Had President Garfield lived longer than the three and a half months after he took office, it is probable that he and his wife, Lucretia, would have preserved at the White House many of the historical objects that were later sold. The Garfields had begun research on the project only two months after they moved to the mansion and had asked the Library of Congress for its aid in tracing the history of the White House and its contents.

Both the Garfields were well educated and could not have been left untouched by the renewed interest in the nation's history that developed after the centennial celebration in Philadelphia. Obviously, they believed that the artifacts that represent history are as important as the events.

Fig. 22 Drawing of White House china collection, made in 1908, shows fruit basket and plate from Grant china and two pieces from the Garfield china. (*From The Century Magazine, October, 1908. Drawing by Harry Fenn. Photograph by Charles Klamkin.*)

President Garfield's short and tragic term of office is not represented in the China Room by any china purchased for use in the White House. There are, however, several of the Garfields' family plates made by Haviland at Limoges in the White House china collection. One pattern is white, with a buff border edged in a gold band. The monogram "G" is on the rim. In contrast with the Hayes plates, those belonging to the Garfields are formal and elegant but simple, and they represent the conservative good taste of James and Lucretia Garfield. (See Fig. 22, Plate 21.)

CHAPTER 22

Chester Alan Arthur
1881–1885

Chester Arthur had none of the Hayeses' and Garfields' sense of history about the White House and saw only a run-down, oversize house filled with Victorian clutter. Undaunted at finding himself the occupant of the President's house, Arthur flatly refused to move into it until he was given money to fix it up. The fastidious widower told Congress, "I will not live in a house looking this way. If Congress does not make an appropriation, I will go ahead and have it done and pay for it out of my own pocket."

Obviously believing that cleanliness came before history, Arthur had twenty-four wagonloads of "decayed furniture" moved out of the White House and sent to Duncanson Brothers, Auctioneers, Ninth and D Street, N.W., to be put up for sale to the general public. There have been reports that the auction was held on the White House lawn, but this is not true. Although it was the rule rather than the exception that White House furnishings which were not wanted would be sold at auction or to secondhand dealers, the Arthur auction brought more publicity than any previous sales because it was so large. Articles ranging from "the trap that caught the rat that ate President Lincoln's coat" to dented pots and pans were sold to a crowd of 5,000 relic seekers. A total of $6,000 was raised for articles that now would be worth many times that sum providing they came with White House provenance. A great many of the plates from previous administrations that were sold at the Arthur auction were the beginnings of many private collections of Presidential china.

President Arthur was not forced to pay for the renovation of the White House "out of his own pocket." Congress appropriated funds for a complete redecoration of the building, and Arthur, a man who was current with the latest fashions in dress and decoration, hired Louis Comfort Tiffany, the New York society decorator. Tiffany, as yet untouched by the Art Nouveau style that was to influence the entire area of the decorative arts, was aware of the ideas of William Morris of England and his Arts and Crafts movement and the elegance of late Victorian decoration. Therefore, the early nineteenth-century building was transformed into a showplace representing all that was new and fashionable in late nineteenth-century decor.

The White House was more "modernized" than it had ever been before. All vestiges of the "old fashioned" were removed, and new-style objects, including pomegranate plush upholstery and large stained-glass wall screens were installed. The Blue Room was painted robin's-egg blue. The commission was Tiffany's big moment, and he spared nothing. Each detail in the mansion was brought up to date, and by the time Arthur felt the building fit to move into, the place shone with colored lights and gilded papers.

Chester Arthur, a widower of only a year when he became President, was a fashionable dresser in spite of his small-town upbringing. He was meticulous in his clothing and in his entertaining. Small, intimate gourmet dinners were given by Arthur in the White House family dining room, which had received Arthur's most careful attention in the refurnishing. The room was resplendent with gold wallpaper and red light fixtures. The stacks of old plates that had been sold at auction were replaced with contemporary porcelain chosen by the President with great care as to fashion and pattern. The White House China Room displays four Chester Arthur dessert plates, each of which is a different pattern. One of the plates is decorated with gold thistles; another has a large rose as its decoration; a third is decorated with cupids; and the fourth is an elaborate adaptation of the Japanese Imari pattern.

The two Arthur plates from private collections illustrated here are typical of the china that was being made in the late nineteenth century. The plate with the scalloped rim and decorated with stylized red and tan flowers was obviously chosen to be used in the family dining room. The blue and gold dinner plate with an elaborate adaptation of the Meissen Onion pattern is certainly "of the period" and is illustrative of Chester Arthur's taste for the contemporary. There is little question that Arthur felt it benefitted the President of the United States to be a leader of what was then considered advanced taste in decorating and entertaining. (See Plates 21, 22.)

CHAPTER 23

Grover Cleveland
1885–1889, 1893–1897

Grover Cleveland was a bachelor when he was elected President in 1885. His sister, Rose, an intelligent and educated woman, was White House hostess until June 2, 1886, when her middle-aged brother married the twenty-two-year-old daughter of his late law partner.

Frances Folsom, called "Frank" by her rotund husband, entertained large crowds frequently in the White House. Large receptions, levees, teas, and

g. 23   Photograph, taken in 1908, of china selected by Mrs. Grover Cleveland. (*From The Century Magazine, October, 1908.*)

luncheons were held, and the young bride made everyone feel welcome. Cleveland and Miss Folsom were married in the Blue Room of the White House, where the President felt they would be allowed more privacy than if they were married elsewhere.

The elegance of the Cleveland wedding set a pattern for future entertainments of that administration. Lavish floral decoration, elaborate food elaborately served, and an informal atmosphere were reported by the guests. For all the elegance, only forty people witnessed the ceremony.

Until his marriage, Cleveland did little to improve the physical appearance of the White House, described once again as "a sorry mess." Evidently, despite Chester Arthur's fastidiousness, things had not been kept clean during the past administration. The attic was described as being "a terrible mess of junk"; and the basement floor, "a place of rubble." The building was said to be infested with cockroaches.

Grover Cleveland solved the immediate situation in his own way. He purchased a residence, Oak View, outside of Washington, where the Clevelands spent as much time as possible, coming in to the White House for the many receptions and parties.

The following year, the White House did see some renovations, but these involved mainly new paint and wallpaper where necessary. Tiffany's decoration was not disturbed. According to reports, neither were the cockroaches.

The Hayes china was used for guests fortunate enough to have been invited to the Cleveland wedding. It is reported that the White House steward suggested to Cleveland that the Hayes and Arthur china might not be to the young bride's liking. Cleveland, who was more than anxious to please "Frank," ordered a service of Wedgwood dishes, with a decoration of full-blown roses, and cut glass from Corning, New York.

Colonel William Crook, a collector of Presidential china himself, was probably the White House employee who suggested the purchase of new china for Mrs. Cleveland. When Cleveland lost the election for a second term, it was to Crook that Mrs. Cleveland said, "I want you to take good care of all the furniture and ornaments in the house and not let any of them get lost or broken, for I want to find everything just as it is now when we come back again. We are coming back just four years from today."

Mrs. Cleveland was, of course, correct in her prediction. The second Cleveland administration started out in a blaze of glory that was, unfortunately, not to last long. Eighteen ninety-three was the year of the Chicago World's Fair, and the President and his cabinet, with their wives, attended the opening of this event. However, an economic crisis swept the nation that year, and Grover Cleveland was discovered to have cancer of the mouth. This fact and the resultant drastic surgery that had to be performed were kept secret from public and press, and Cleveland was operated on aboard a friend's yacht. That same year the Clevelands' second child, a daughter, was born in the White House.

The young Mrs. Cleveland proved to have a strong character and obviously never neglected her social duties despite her problems. I. W. Hoover, chief usher of the White House during Cleveland's second term of office, wrote, "During this time the old house saw more brilliant entertaining than it has ever witnessed before or since: The dinners, receptions, and other social functions, unusual from every point of view." (See Plate 22.)

One more Cleveland baby was to be born before the administration was over. Two sons were born later. The President, who had been 48 years old when he married Frances Folsom, survived his illness by fifteen years. Although she was very young when she assumed her duties as First Lady, Frances Folsom Cleveland was an outstanding wife, mother, and hostess.

CHAPTER 24

Benjamin Harrison
1889–1893

The Harrison administration has been described as a most simple and homelike affair all the way through. Children, grandchildren, and in-laws were constant visitors at the White House. Each day was run on a strict routine, with meals at regular hours.

The White House was again said to be a mess and to need many repairs. Caroline Harrison, a dedicated housekeeper, began to agitate for a new residence for the Presidential family. This was not a new idea, and under the Harrison administration, the plan got as far as a model being built; but the scheme was abandoned because of lack of public support. Mrs. Harrison consoled herself by remodeling the White House. New bathrooms were built, and the kitchen was completely torn out and remodeled. Electric lights were installed. The modernization under the Harrison administration was accomplished with a congressional appropriation of $35,000, and it was generally felt that Mrs. Harrison's careful spending made this sum go far.

Mrs. Harrison, the daughter of a Presbyterian minister, saw to it that the family began each day with a prayer meeting in the family quarters. Benjamin Harrison was as rigid and straight-laced as his wife. The First Lady had a passion for flowers, most particularly orchids, and the neglected White House conservatory was rebuilt and added to. All rooms were painted, and the family living quarters were divided into suites.

White House entertainments, although not held often during the Harrison administration, were lavish in food and decoration. Floral displays were elaborate and in high Victorian style. Described as "unpretentious," Mrs. Harrison had a reputation for being a warm hostess and was the popular first president general of the newly organized Daughters of the American Revolution.

Caroline Harrison's interest in china decoration went back to her earlier life in Indianapolis, where she had taught china painting to young ladies. She often painted flowers, most particularly orchids, on plates and presented these as gifts to her friends.

Fig. 24 Drawing of Harrison plates and a goblet from the White House china collection in 1908. (*From The Century Magazine, October, 1908. Drawing by Harry Fenn. Photograph by Charles Klamkin.*)

During the general cleanup of the White House, many of the remnants of dinner services of former administrations came to light. Caroline Harrison is to be credited with saving the remains of many dinner services of historical interest. She had a china restorer visit the White House periodically. Before this time, broken, chipped, or cracked plates had been sold or thrown out; now these were mended and preserved for Mrs. Harrison's dream of having a White House china collection. By this period in American history, several writers had already brought attention to the hobby of china collecting, which had been popular in Europe for many years. It had not yet really caught on as a hobby in America. Historically, the time was right for attention to be paid to these sadly neglected White House relics.

It is not surprising that Mrs. Harrison designed the decoration for her own state china. Delicate china patterns were the vogue by this time, and the overdecorated Hayes service looked out of date. However, it is not unlikely that Mrs. Harrison, had she liked the Hayes china, would have left a legacy of her own china in the White House in any case.

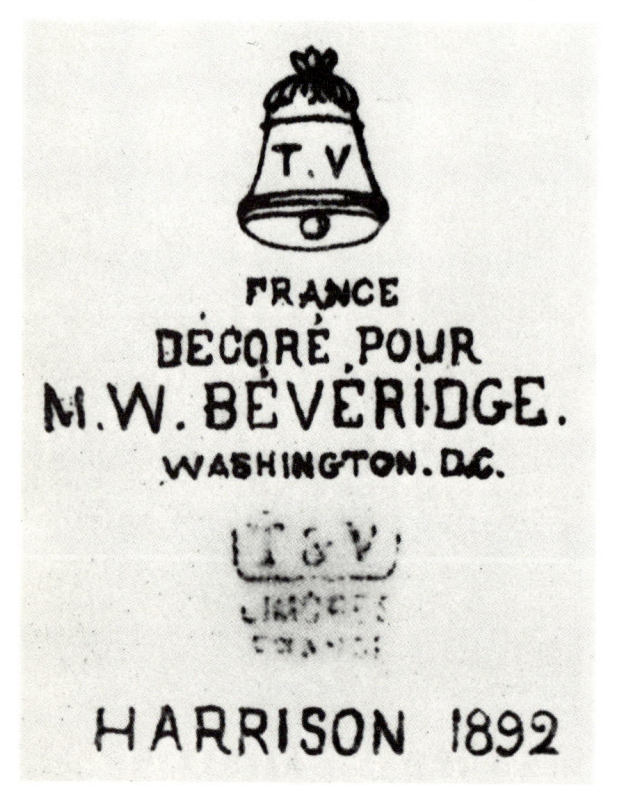

Fig. 25 Mark on reverse of Harrison china, showing store in Washington that sold it. The name and date of Presidential administration were printed on the plate in an attempt to ward off souvenir seekers. (*Photograph by Charles Klamkin*)

The design Mrs. Harrison chose was derivative of the Lincoln china. The design combines two motifs of goldenrod and leaf with Indian corn and stalk in flat gold over the underglaze blue rim of each plate. An inner border of forty-four gold stars representing the number of states then in the Union sets off the coat of arms in the center. This center motif was adapted from the Lincoln china. In order to discourage souvenir hunters, Mrs. Harrison had "Harrison 1892" stamped on the reverse of each plate. (See Fig. 25.)

Similar motifs were used to varying degrees on the different kinds of plates in the Harrison service. Some plates have the border colors reversed. The Harrison service was made by the Limoges firm of Tresseman and Vogt, which had been in business for ten years. They made the whiteware and decorated it with Mrs. Harrison's designs. (See Fig. 24, Plates 4, 22, 23.)

Caroline Harrison obviously never got an opportunity to enjoy her own china. The lady who had gathered the beginnings of the White House china collection and housed it in new cabinets for display to tourists, died the year her own china was delivered. Enough plates of the Harrison set still survive and are used occasionally for small dinners at the White House.

CHAPTER 25

William McKinley
1897–1901

The administration of William McKinley was marked by the tenure of another ailing First Lady. Mrs. McKinley was the victim of epilepsy, an affliction never discussed in polite society at the turn of the century. Protocol at state dinners was changed so that on the occasions when his wife was well enough to attend, McKinley sat her next to him. When Mrs. McKinley went into one of her "fainting spells" at the table, McKinley would place a handkerchief over her face until she had recovered.

Extremely solicitous of his sick wife, McKinley exerted little pressure on her in the way of social obligations. The White House was said to "run itself" through the McKinley years. The public adored McKinley for his concerned attitude toward his wife. However, during the campaign, political opponents made much of the fact that were Mrs. McKinley to be First Lady, there would be no hostess for White House social functions.

The McKinley years saw no decline in the elegance that had become the White House style of entertaining. Although little imagination was used in the menus, as many as seventy-one courses were served, as on the occasion when Sanford B. Dole, president of Hawaii, and his wife were honored at a state dinner.

While Mrs. McKinley knitted in her room, President McKinley arranged the social functions and even saw to the orders for floral decorations. The one function that Mrs. McKinley seems to have arranged was an entertainment in commemoration of the centennial of White House occupancy by John Adams, held on December 12, 1900.

Mrs. McKinley, protected and cared for, showed remarkable reserves of strength when her husband was shot. She survived him by six years.

The Harrison china, delivered at the end of that administration, must have been used during the McKinley administration. Although the service designed for Mrs. Harrison was certainly used at State occasions, the tea service illustrated here, said to be Mrs. McKinley's favorite, is represented in the China Room at the White House. It was made by Haviland at Limoges and has a border of roses inside an outer border of gold and blue. Another McKinley plate in the White House collection has a blue-green rim overlaid with a gold pattern. The McKinley taste in china seems to have run to simple, neat patterns on porcelain of the Dresden or Meissen type. (See Plate 23.)

CHAPTER 26

Theodore Roosevelt
1901–1909

Theodore Roosevelt was a President noted for many firsts. He was the first Chief Executive to ride in an automobile, the youngest man to take the oath of office as President of the United States, the first President to fly in an airplane, the first American President to visit a foreign country while in office, the first American recipient of a Nobel Prize, and the first President to order Wedgwood state china for the White House.

The Executive Mansion was an exciting house during the Roosevelt administration. Five lively children, according to Bess Furman in *White House Profile*, historian of White House occupants and festivities, "had parties, collected menageries, [and] walked on tall stilts over White House stairways and upper halls."

Theodore Roosevelt's second wife, Edith Carow Roosevelt, was an exceptional manager who was capable of keeping the active family in tow and making social events in the mansion run smoothly. Many entertainments took place in honor of Alice, the President's daughter by his first marriage, who is still *grande dame* of Washington society. Miss Roosevelt's marriage to Nicholas Longworth on February 17, 1906, was the highpoint of White House social activity during the

Theodore Roosevelt administration. The wedding was attended by more than one thousand guests, but Miss Alice chose to be attended by no one. The groom, however, had eight ushers and a best man.

After existing for over one hundred years, the White House was ready for a complete renovation by the turn of the century. When Roosevelt had been in office only a few weeks, Congress voted $475,445 for the purpose of repairing and refurnishing the Executive Mansion. Roosevelt was also given an additional $65,196 to build a west wing to be used as executive offices. For the first time in its existence, the mansion became solely the residence of the Presidential family, and the business offices were removed to the adjoining wing. The Victorian greenhouses and conservatory were torn down to make room for the addition.

While the work was being done, the Roosevelt family lived in a house on the west side of Lafayette Square. Alice Roosevelt Longworth described the state of the White House before the renovation as "late General Grant and early Pullman." The east and west wings, as originally planned by Thomas Jefferson, were restored. Original mantels, which had been removed and placed in storage, were put back in their former spots; and many pieces of furniture from previous administrations were brought out of storage, restored, and used again.

Once Roosevelt had moved into his new executive offices, it became apparent that a new state dinner service would be needed as part of the furnishings for the renovated house. He could not believe that it would be impossible to find a suitable dinner service that could be manufactured in the United States. "Is it possible? Is it possible," he is reported to have asked his secretary, "that we are dependent upon foreign factories for the very dishes upon which the Chief Executives of the United States must eat?" In disbelief, Roosevelt had his agents search the entire country for a pottery which could produce a dinner service that would provide enough plates for a party of 100 persons. The state of the art of porcelain manufacture in America was still in its infancy at the time, and it did not take long before Roosevelt was convinced that no one in this country was capable of providing a dinner service of suitable size or quality for the President's table. At that point in the history of the American ceramic industry, there was such popular resistance to American pottery that domestic potters used foreign labels and European marks in order to compete in the market place.

Fortunately for Roosevelt, a superb quality of bone china was being produced in Etruria, England, by the factory established in the eighteenth century by Josiah Wedgwood. An earlier abortive attempt by Josiah's son at producing china had lasted only a few years (1812–1822), and it was not until 1878 that the famous pottery had been able to produce bone china and market it successfully. The new Wedgwood china was extremely strong, despite its fragile appearance, and it was an especially good choice as a state dinner service for the White House. (See Fig. 26.)

The Roosevelt china was ordered by the President in 1902 and was delivered a year later. It was decorated by Herbert Cholerton, decorator, artist, heraldic painter, and gilder, who worked for Wedgwood between the years 1901 and 1955. The shapes for the Roosevelt china were specially designed by John E. Goodwin, art director for Wedgwood between 1902 and 1934. The Wedgwood bone china chosen by Roosevelt is copyrighted and patented for exclusive use in the White House. A similar pattern, without the Great Seal of the United States, called "Gold Colonnade," is still being produced by Wedgwood. However, the patent would preclude any of the Roosevelt service being reproduced for general sale to the public, as had happened in the case of the Haviland Limoges services of previous administrations. The total order was for 1,296 pieces and the Wedgwood design number was X5333. (See Plate 24.)

It is hardly surprising that, unlike other White House dinner services, very little of the Roosevelt Wedgwood has found its way to private collections. The reason for this can best be explained when one examines the posthumously published letters of Archie Butt, White House historian for the last eleven months of the Roosevelt administration. In addition to his official duties as historian, Butt managed to keep a personal record of White House happenings by writing copious letters to his mother and, following her death, to his sister-in-law, Mrs. Lewis F. Butt.

In a letter dated December 11, 1908, written to "Dear Clara," Butt records the First Lady's attitude toward the disposal of chipped, cracked, or broken china:

> I had rather an interesting time the last few days looking over the china at the White House with a view to destroying all that is chipped or broken in any way. Mrs. Roosevelt does not want it sold at auction, for

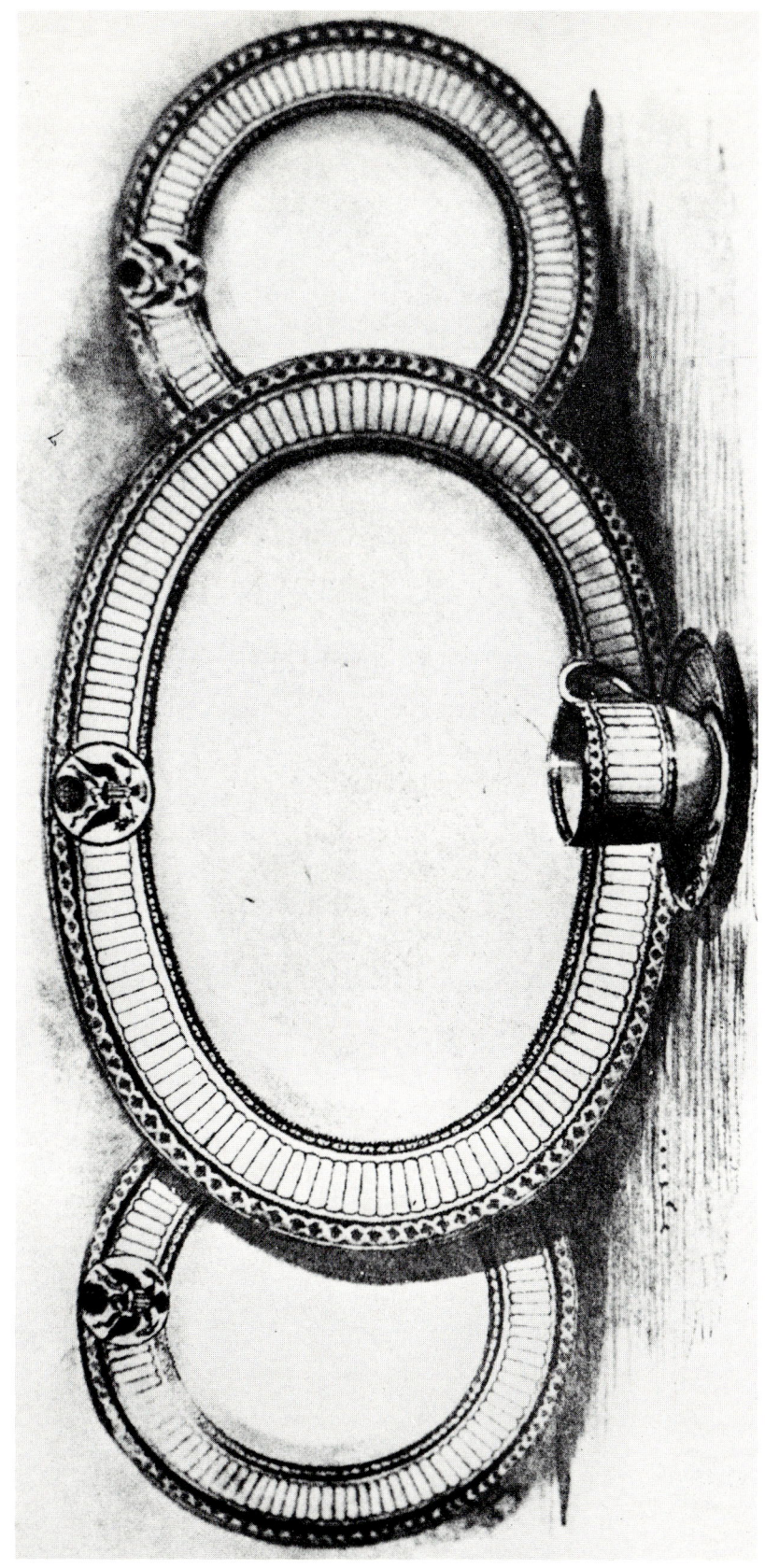

Fig. 26 Drawing of White House china selected for collection by Mrs. Theodore Roosevelt when she organized china collection with Abby Gunn Baker. (*From The Century Magazine, October, 1908. Drawing by Harry Fenn. Photograph by Charles Klamkin.*)

she thinks this method cheapens the White House. I took the matter up with Bromwell, who really has it on his papers and is responsible for it, and he thought it ought to be sold by private bids to cabinet officers and others who are connected with the White House in some way. In former years it was regarded as the property of the mistress of the White House, who would give it away as she desired, but Mrs. R. thinks that it should never be given away—and it should not, in my opinion, for it is government property just the same as the furniture. If it were sold by private bids it would create an awful howl in the press, should it become known, and so I convinced all concerned that it should be broken up and scattered in the river, which will be done. When I think how I should value even one piece of it it hurts to smash it, but I am sure it is the only right thing to do.

Mother was accustomed to say that when one was in doubt what to do, it were well to stop to think how it would look in the newspapers and act accordingly. She said that even a mother would forgive what the public would not condone, and so it was not always safe to measure one's actions by what one's mother would think. It is a test I often put myself to, and it has kept me from doing some questionable things in the service, and I think it was that standard as much as anything else which kept me free from the petty scandals in the Philippines.

I ran across one plate in a pawnshop the other day which, if I am rightly informed, was one of the Grant set. The owner wanted fifty dollars for it. Sloan, the auctioneer, tells me that he would be able to get from ten to fifty dollars for every plate which the White House would sell and badly broken pieces would bring something.

Mrs. Roosevelt has collected nearly all the china of past administrations, which is now in the cabinets in the White House. She has had some pieces donated to her, and others she has purchased at very high prices. Of course, she paid for them out of the contingent expenses of the White House and they belong to the Government, but if she had not interested herself in collecting what remained of the china of former administrations it is doubtful if it would ever have been done. In order to insure the continuance of their care she has donated them to the Smithsonian Institution, but to be kept in the White House crypt as long as it is desired to leave them there. This means that the Smithsonian Institution is responsible for them and takes stock of the collection at regular intervals.

Regardless of Mrs. Roosevelt's insurance that the china collection would be cared for and added to, if it were not for succeeding First Ladies who interested themselves in the collection, it might still have suffered from neglect.

CHAPTER 27

William Howard Taft
1909–1913

Foul weather ushered in the four-year administration of William Howard and Helen Taft. On the morning of the inauguration Mrs. Taft ignored precedent and insisted on riding back to the White House with her husband. Helen Herron Taft had played a strong role in her husband's political career and she was not about to take a back seat on the day he was made President of the United States.

Taft was well aware of the political advantages of entertaining at the White House, and during his tariff fights with Congress, the President began a custom of politicking at his own parties. Archie Butt recorded that during this period, "He used the White House as a great political adjunct to the battle." When the President's bills finally passed, the Tafts held a "harmony dinner" for all those who had championed the President's cause.

Helen Taft, who had been hostess at many successful social evenings during her years in Manila, began the first White House social season of her husband's administration by energetically fulfilling her duties. Archie Butt wrote that every senator and most of the important members of the House had been entertained. "In addition to this she had planned and carried through two big garden parties and innumerable smaller affairs." However, only ten weeks after the inauguration, she suffered a stroke, probably from overwork, and was left with a paralysis of the face. Although she worked to overcome the resultant speech problem, her performance as First Lady was hampered throughout the remainder of her husband's term of office. During Mrs. Taft's illness, four of her sisters took turns being hostess at White House entertainments. President Taft assumed some of the burden, and he already had a reputation for being a genial host.

Mrs. Taft conceived an idea of turning Potomac Park into a promenade where "all Washington could meet, either on foot or in vehicles, at five o'clock on certain evenings." She arranged to have two bandstands built, and concerts were given. She also had 80 cherry trees planted along the banks of the river, and later in the same year, 2,000 more trees were sent to Washington as a gift from the city of Tokyo. This first shipment was burned when the Department of Agriculture found them to be diseased, and Japan sent 3,000 new trees, which were planted in 1912.

Helen Taft had her own ideas of how the White House should be run, and she was the first First Lady to hire a housekeeper. She said, "I wanted a woman who could relieve me of the supervision of such details as no man, expert steward though he may be, would ever recognize." Mrs. Elizabeth Jaffray was the woman who replaced the White House steward.

Three cooks were in charge of the elaborate multicourse meals served in the Taft household. Taft himself was a heavy eater. In spite of the large amount of entertaining, Mrs. Taft was an excellent manager, and she kept food bills to a minimum. She purchased a cow to provide milk for her family, ordered food in bulk, and insisted that no out-of-season food be served. Further economies, according to Mr. Ike Hoover, who worked at the White House, included the closing off of many of the White House rooms.

Mrs. Taft also reduced the staff of servants and replaced police guards with uniformed black footmen. After her many years of living in a warm climate, Helen Taft enjoyed outdoor entertaining and had red shades placed on the outside light fixtures. Poor weather and insects led to the statement by Mr. Hoover that Mrs. Taft's outdoor parties were "jinxed."

One of the outstanding social events held by the Tafts at the White House was their silver wedding anniversary party, celebrated with a night garden party on June 19, 1911. Five thousand guests were present, and Archie Butt called it "the most brilliant function ever held" at the White House.

Although the Tafts were not too popular with their household staff or with Washington society, Mrs. Taft, in her book *Recollections of Full Years,* manages to excuse her zealousness as a housekeeper while she was First Lady:

> The members of my family, and especially my children, are prone to indulgence in good-natured personalities and they like to make the most of my serious attitude toward my domestic responsibilities, saying that I make them three times as difficult as they need be by too positive insistance on my own methods.
>
> Perhaps I did make the process of adjusting the White House routine to my own conceptions a shade too strenuous, but I could not feel that I was mistress of any house if I did not take an active interest in all the details of running it.

White House servants charged that Mrs. Taft had her face in all the pots and pans and would not stay out of the kitchen.

Of the White House china, Mrs. Taft wrote,

> Mrs. Roosevelt, as the retiring mistress of the White House, naturally would make no changes or purchases which might not meet with the approval of her successor, so I found the linen supply depleted, the table service inadequate through breakages, and other furnishing necessary. There is a government appropriation to meet the expense of such replenishments and repairs, and every President's wife is supposed to avail herself of any part of it she requires to fit the mansion for her own occupancy.
>
> Perhaps nothing in the house is so expressive of the various personalities of its Mistresses as the dinner services which each has contributed. For my part I was entirely satisfied with the quiet taste displayed by Mrs. Roosevelt and contented myself with filling up the different broken sets in her service to the number necessary for one hundred covers.

Helen Taft said that she always enjoyed using some of the historic old plates and platters at small luncheons and dinners. At the time, there were enough plates left of the Lincoln service to use for one course. She said that although she spoke of the different china patterns as expressive of the personalities they represented, they probably were even more representative of popular taste rather than individual preference. Mrs. Taft noted, "Samples of all the different services, displayed in cabinets in the long eastern corridor, are among the most interesting exhibits in the White House."

She did not dislike the hunting trophies left on White House walls by Teddy Roosevelt, and she was also happy with the redecoration undertaken by the previous administration.

The Monroe centerpiece was used often during the Taft administration. Of it, Mrs. Taft wrote:

> For any dinner under sixty I was able to use a large oval top which could be extended by the carpenters to almost any size. On this table I used the massive silver-gilt ornaments which President Monroe imported from France along with his interesting collection of French porcelains, clocks and statuettes which still occupy many cabinets and mantels here and there in the house.
>
> These ornaments remind one of the Cellini period when silversmiths vied with each other in elaborations.

She described the *surtout* and its various accessories and then said, "In their way they are exceedingly handsome, and they certainly are appropriate to the ceremony with which a state dinner at the White House is usually conducted."

On January 11, 1913, a dinner was held for Mrs. Cleveland, who had just announced her engagement to Professor Preston of Princeton. Mrs. Cleveland's favorite flowers, jonquils and pansies, were used on the table; and Mr. Hoover described the table as set with the "beautiful red-bordered plate" that Mrs. Cleveland had selected herself just eighteen years before.

The Roosevelt china that Helen Taft said she "filled in" was, of course, the Wedgwood bone china described and illustrated in Chapter 26. Since a large amount of this set was ordered in 1912, it is probable that it was used for a rather long period in the White House.

The Wedgwood creamware plate illustrated in this chapter is an authentic White House plate and was probably ordered as everyday china for the White House. Staffordshire ironstone and a Minton dessert service are also included in the Taft display in the china collection. (See Plate 25.)

CHAPTER 28

Woodrow Wilson
1913–1921

Woodrow Wilson was the first President to purchase American-made state china for the White House. Although other Presidents had tried to find suitable American plates, there had not previously been an American potter able to supply a dinner service of good quality in the large amount required. The establishment of the Lenox Pottery in Trenton, New Jersey, and their capability of producing fine vitrified china with characteristics similar to those of Irish Belleek finally made it possible for an American President and his guests to eat from domestic china.

Because subsequent Presidential dinner services have, with few exceptions, been made by Lenox, it is proper here to give some of the history of how that firm became established in a country that had had little history of making good-quality ceramics. There was little acceptance by the American public of home-made porcelain, and by far the largest amount of china purchased in nineteenth-century America was produced abroad. The desire for only foreign pottery and porcelain had led some of the American potters to label their goods as foreign, with the hope that they would find more acceptance on the market. Lenox set out to produce a quality of china that would equal or surpass the foreign competitors' products and stated that "no false labels shall ever be used on Lenox dishes."

Fig. 27 Dinner plate from Wilson service. Reverse shows mark and date. This same state china was used through the Wilson, Harding, Coolidge, and Hoover administrations. (*The Smithsonian Institution*)

Walter Scott Lenox was blind and crippled by the time he had perfected his china. He was assisted in his work by Harry A. Brown, secretary to the company, who directed the factory and reported all progress to Lenox. The culmination of all Lenox's efforts was the order from President Wilson for state china for White House use. The service was completed only a few months before Lenox's death. (See Fig. 27.)

Each plate of the Wilson service has an ivory border and a cream-white center. The plates have a border decoration of stars and stripes in formal arrangement etched in gold. At the top of each plate, in the border, is the President's seal. Frank G. Holmes, chief artist of the Lenox Pottery, designed the service. President Wilson suggested using the President's seal rather than the national coat of arms, which Holmes had originally wanted, since the dishes were for use in the President's home. The seal was used with the eagle's head turned toward the bundle of arrows to indicate wartime. The service plates of Wilson china are rimmed in a deep, brilliant blue. The outer border, in gold, has an urn and scroll motif.

In order to be certain that the first American-made state china would not go unnoticed by the press, Abby Gunn Baker, who had already written many articles about the White House china collection, was asked to write a press release describing the new purchase. Miss Baker began her article by stating, "The proud day has arrived at last when the United States is the possessor of a White House state dining service which was designed by an American artist, was made from American clay at an American pottery, burned at American kilns and decorated by American workmen. From the largest dish to the smallest, every piece of this new china, which has just been delivered at the White House is American made."

Mrs. Baker, to whom credit must be given for gathering the first display of Presidential china under the direction of Mrs. McKinley and then of Mrs. Roosevelt, goes on to say that

> few realize the work involved in securing a state dining set for the White House. Months were consumed in the preparation of designs for the present service. Pattern after pattern was made and discarded. Both the President and Mrs. Wilson wanted something as fine as could be produced in

the European potteries, primarily because it was to be the first American made dining set, and for that reason must be above criticism. They wanted it also to be exceedingly simple, and in these war times they were especially desirous that the decorations should have a patriotic motif.

Fig. 28 Lenox service plate and bouillon cup and saucer from Wilson state dinner service. (*Photograph, courtesy of Lenox, Inc.*)

In round numbers the service will comprise seventeen hundred pieces, and each piece is in two tints, a deep ivory border and the cream white china in the center of the dish. There will be no color in any of the decorations save the service plates.

The decorations are in rolled gold. Each flat piece is edged with a narrow border of the stars and stripes, and at the top of each is a conception of the President's seal.

The tea cups and the little after dinner coffee cups bear golden handles and are decorated with the same design as the plates. The flaring ramekins, the double handled bouillon cups, the breakfast food dishes and the little bowls to hold the relish for the oyster cocktail in the oyster plates bear the same decorations.

The large chop plates, which will be used also as cake servers, have a narrow rim of the ivory tint on which the design is painted, while the body of the plate is the cream white fabric. The service plate is the most beautiful plate of its kind which ever graced the White House.

The border of the plate is of an indescribable deep blue, darker than the Wedgewood [Mrs. Baker never did learn the proper spelling of this word] and yet more brilliant. It is bordered in gold in an etching of the Adam period, including an Adam urn and scroll. The inner border bears the Stars and Stripes. The handsome seal stands directly in the center of the plate and attracts the eye at first glance. The plate measures eleven inches instead of the usual ten and a half and thus enables the beauty of the decoration to be seen while it carries a soup or an entree plate.

Mrs. Baker concludes this enthusiastic description of the Wilson service by describing the china as "of marvelous strength and fibre, and it is built to bear long usage." The service was named the "President Wilson Design." (See Fig. 28, Plate 25.)

While articles in the press lauded President Wilson's support of an American industry, another purchase of china by the Wilsons received little attention and seems not to have been recorded by either the White House or the Smithsonian Institution. This china is perhaps even more of a memorial than the Lenox to a President who struggled for an international organization for the preservation of peace in the world. This china was made by Wedgwood during World War I, and its design, production, and sale were due to the efforts of Mrs. Robert Coleman Taylor of New York. (See Plate 25.)

Mrs. Taylor, an American Anglophile, first got the idea for the "Liberty

China" before America entered World War I, and the purpose of selling the china was to raise money for "war sufferers." Mrs. Taylor, in a booklet she wrote and published privately in 1924, stated that she had decided to have commemorated "this chapter in our history" before we had entered the war and that she "was ready when the President sent his message to Congress."

In deciding to perpetuate the important event of the war in history, Mrs. Taylor thought that patriotic china would be a fitting memorial and that the china should be made by a great potter. Her hope was that Josiah Wedgwood and Sons of Etruria, England, would manufacture the china and that William H. Plummer and Company of New York would "help with the business of importing and delivering it." She stipulated to Mr. Plummer that the china was a private order, was never to be advertised, that the samples would be shown only in Mrs. Taylor's drawing room, and that when peace was declared the orders would cease. "The war china would stop with the war." All profits would go for war relief work.

Mrs. Taylor designed the china herself. The design consisted of the American shield in the midst of the Allied flags, with the flags of England and France at the top, the flag of Belgium between them, and a wreath of laurel to surround the shield. The decoration was to be kept small and used as a coat of arms; the only other decoration was a narrow band of gold on the edges. Mrs. Taylor chose the name "Liberty china."

The Liberty pattern was used on both bone china and Queen's ware, and with few exceptions, only tea sets and dessert sets were made. The orders far exceeded delivery, and since the china was only sold "from tea-table to tea-table," it is remarkable that the design and the china became internationally known.

Mrs. Taylor recorded that "surprisingly little of the china was lost in transit. On the ocean every month of the war the submarines never caught a piece." The total of pieces of Liberty china made and delivered was 9,251, and the project raised $14,203.14 for the war charities.

The copper plates for the design were, at Mrs. Taylor's request, destroyed personally by Major Wedgwood at the end of the war. It was at this time that Wedgwood suggested that Mrs. Taylor prepare a small booklet for private circulation, telling the whole story of the wartime china. "We shall hope to obtain one of these copies from you, when it will be stored in the archives of our Museum as one of the few pleasant memories of the sad and terrible war." The booklet was published in a limited edition of 1,000.

Mrs. Taylor lists in her account the many charities that received benefits of her unique wartime project. Fortunately, all purchasers of the Liberty china are named in the booklet. Two of the purchasers listed under the District of Columbia are the President and Mrs. Wilson. Liberty china was considered extremely fashionable and patriotic among the relatively few people who had been privileged to purchase it. It is also very attractive, and there is little doubt that the tea services ordered by the President and his wife were used at the White House during World War I.

CHAPTER 29

Warren Gamaliel Harding
1921–1923

The Harding administration was not the happiest either for the country or for the Hardings. Despite the Hardings' domestic problems, a great amount of elegant entertaining was done at the White House during that administration. Huge garden parties and ostentatious dinners were given. Washington social life returned to normal after Wilson's wartime austerity. President Harding entertained his cronies at stag luncheons and breakfasts.

Although the Harding administration was beset by the poor health and unhappy marriage of the President and the First Lady, Florence Kling Harding found the time and energy to have the White House silverware gold-plated to match the Monroe *surtout*. These accessories were used with the Wilson china on state occasions.

Mrs. Harding took little personal interest in the position she held as hostess of the White House when it came to planning the dinners and receptions. The White House staff and outside caterers managed the large affairs with little direction from her. The First Lady, called "The Duchess" by her husband, was described by one White House employee as "wild and anxious." It was said that she "could not be a social success." Entertainments at the White House, no

PLATE 21

Above Buff-bordered family plate, made by Haviland, for President and Mrs. Garfield. (*The Smithsonian Institution*)

Above Elaborate plate from Chester Arthur administration, with blue and gold decoration on white porcelain. (*Collection of Marjorie W. Hardy. Photograph by Charles Klamkin.*)

Below Soup plate, Royal Worcester, is registered and dated and was probably purchased by Chester Arthur to match decoration in the family dining room at the White House. (*Collection of Marjorie W. Hardy. Photograph by Charles Klamkin.*)

Above Maroon, pink, and buff stylized floral decoration on the Chester Arthur plate is indicative of the President's passion for the contemporary style of his period. (*Collection of Marjorie W. Hardy. Photograph by Charles Klamkin.*)

PLATE 22

Above Chester Arthur was said to have ordered plates "with great roses in the border." It is probable that this White House plate dates from the Arthur administration. (*Private collection. Photograph by Charles Klamkin.*)

Above right Small porcelain saucer said to have been used by Grover Cleveland while he was governor of New York. (*Collection of Marjorie W. Hardy. Photograph by Charles Klamkin.*)

Right Creamware plate with border of roses, probably from the set purchased by Cleveland for his bride at the suggestion of White House employees. (*Private collection. Photograph by Charles Klamkin.*)

Below Harrison plates and cup and saucer designed by Mrs. Harrison and made and decorated at Limoges, France. (*The Smithsonian Institution*)

PLATE 23

Left China designed by and made for Mrs. Benjamin Harrison is displayed in mahogany breakfront in the White House. (*White House Historical Association. Photograph by National Geographic Society.*)

Above Dinner plate of Harrison state china. (*Private collection. Photograph by Charles Klamkin.*)

Right Haviland cup and saucer with cobalt blue and gold border is a pattern alternately called "McKinley" and "Cleveland" in White House display. This pattern was open stock at the time and, therefore, is difficult to date exactly. (*Collection of Marjorie W. Hardy. Photograph by Charles Klamkin.*)

PLATE 24

Above Two plates and a bouillon cup and saucer from Theodore Roosevelt Wedgwood bone china state dinner service. (*The Smithsonian Institution*)

Above Hand-painted menu cover for dinner given by Theodore Roosevelt for Prince Henry of Prussia. The dinner was stag, and the elaborate decorations were red, white, and blue. Ten courses were served. (*Ralph E. Becker Collection of Political Americana, The Smithsonian Institution. Photograph by Charles Klamkin.*)

Above Porcelain plate with painting of Warwick Castle, previously owned by President and Mrs. Theodore Roosevelt. (*Collection of Marjorie W. Hardy. Photograph by Charles Klamkin.*)

PLATE 25

Above Although Mrs. Taft ordered more Wedgwood bone china in the Roosevelt pattern in 1912, this Wedgwood Queen's ware plate from the White House is dated 1910 and was probably used as a breakfast service or in the family dining room. *(Collection of Marjorie W. Hardy. Photograph by Charles Klamkin.)*

Top right Minton cup and saucer from dessert service owned by Mrs. Taft and used in White House. *(Collection of Marjorie W. Hardy. Photograph by Charles Klamkin.)*

Right Service plate from Woodrow Wilson state china service. This is first American-made dinner service ordered for White House. Made by Lenox. *(The Smithsonian Institution)*

Below Liberty pattern Wedgwood bone china tea service. Both President and Mrs. Wilson ordered this china during World War I. *(Mattatuck Museum, Waterbury, Connecticut. Photograph by Charles Klamkin.)*

PLATE 26

Top Official state china made for Franklin Delano Roosevelt. President Roosevelt helped design the border, which includes motifs from his family coat of arms. *(The Smithsonian Institution)*

Middle Service plate, dinner plate, and cup and saucer from the teal green- and yellow-bordered Truman state dinner service made by Lenox. This set of plates has been used in the White House continually since the Truman administration. *(The Smithsonian Institution)*

Left Eisenhower birthday plate, made in a limited edition to be presented by the President as favors to guests attending the party given for his first birthday spent in the White House. *(Private collection. Photograph by Charles Klamkin.)*

Above Madison china is displayed in White House on top of reproduction of desk on which Monroe Doctrine was signed. Desk was given to the White House collection by Mrs. Herbert Hoover. Small painting is by Albert Bierstadt. Mrs. Kennedy was interested in all historical relics in the White House collection and spent a great amount of effort to see that they would be preserved. *(White House Historical Association. Photograph by National Geographic Society)*

Above President's dining room, built in family quarters of the White House during Kennedy administration. Table is set with Lincoln china. Both Mrs. Kennedy and Mrs. Johnson used historic china from the White House collection for small dinners. *(White House Historical Association. Photograph by National Geographic Society.)*

PLATE 27

Above Dinner and salad plates from the Lyndon B. Johnson state dinner service. *(The Smithsonian Institution)*

PLATE 28

Above Bowls from the Lyndon B. Johnson state china, used for serving and for flower arrangements. *(The Smithsonian Institution)*

Right Reproduction of Washington States plate. Probably made by Haviland. Reproductions of Presidential plates were made for Chicago World's Fair in 1893. These plates are also known to have been reproduced on various Washington commemorative anniversaries. *(Private collection. Photograph by Charles Klamkin.)*

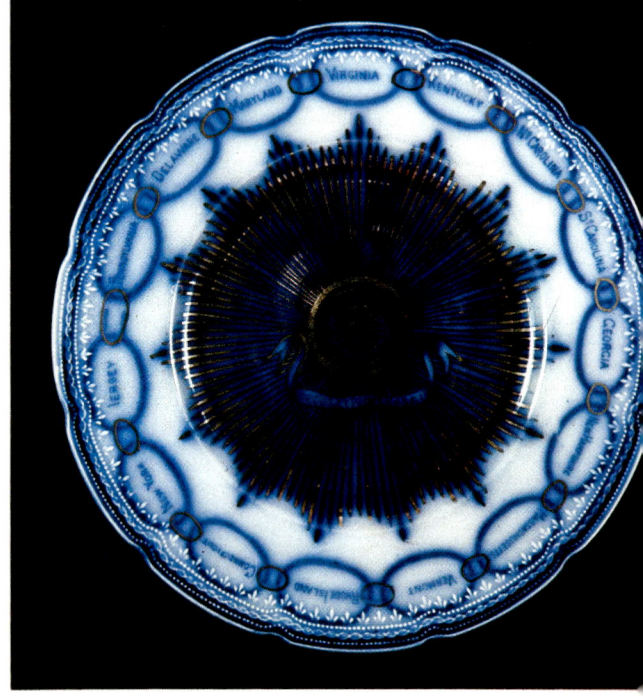

Left Martha Washington States plate. Made by Shenango China Company in 1932 for Washington bicentennial. *(Private collection. Photograph by Charles Klamkin.)*

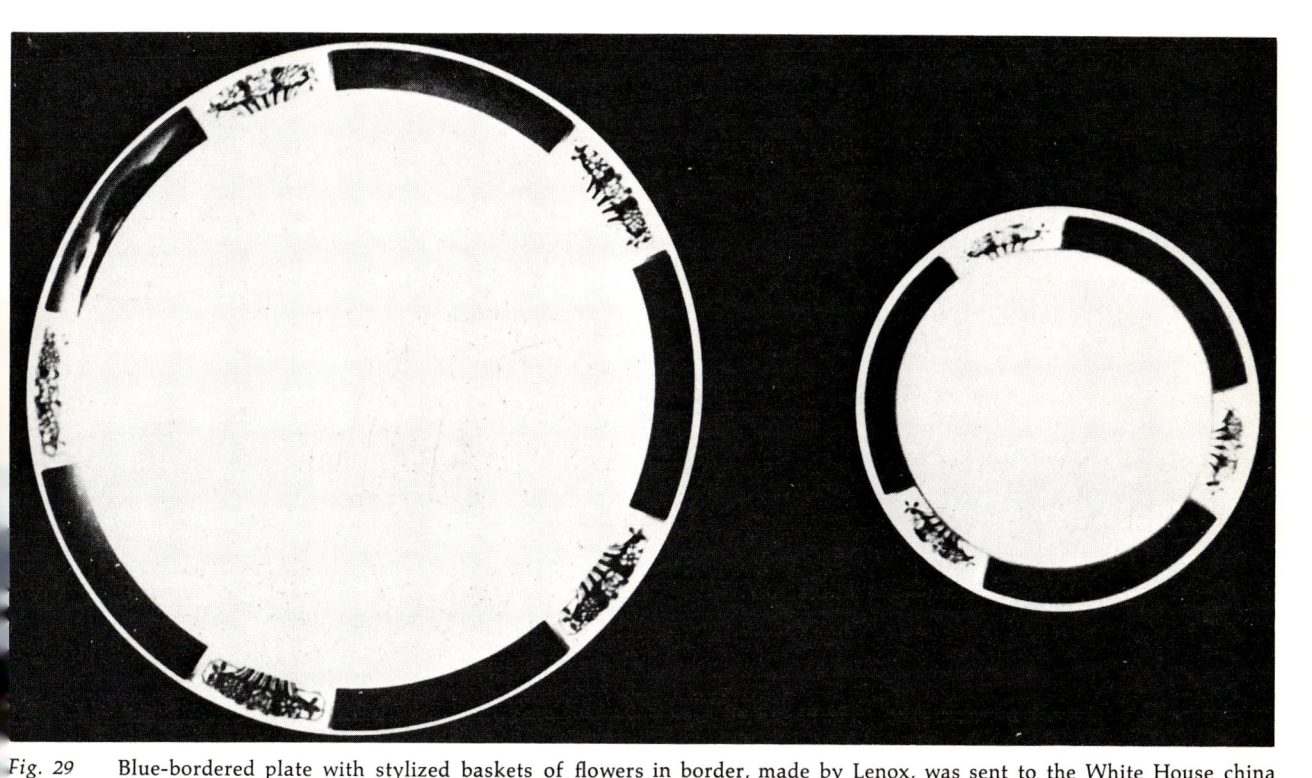

Fig. 29 Blue-bordered plate with stylized baskets of flowers in border, made by Lenox, was sent to the White House china collection by the Harding Home and Museum when Mrs. Eisenhower reorganized China Room in 1959.

matter how elegant, were reported as dull and boring. The Eighteenth Amendment probably added considerably to the atmosphere of gloom that pervaded the White House during the state affairs.

Although the Wilson china was the official state china of the Harding administration, the Harding Home and Museum sent representative china to the White House collection in 1959. A dessert plate and an after-dinner cup and saucer were sent to Mrs. Eisenhower during her reorganization of the china collection. This Harding china is Lenox, and the pattern consists of a narrow blue border with five stylized basket insets. (See Fig. 29.)

121

CHAPTER 30

Calvin Coolidge
1923–1929

Grace Coolidge was a welcome change in the White House. She was said to have "spread sunshine wherever she went," a noticeable departure from the frosty Mrs. Harding. She was an attractive woman who dressed well and became a popular figure in the White House and in Washington society. Calvin Coolidge made most of the household decisions and chose menus and supervised expenses. However, it was the outgoing Mrs. Coolidge who charmed guests and carried on the conversations at the many parties and dinners held at the White House during those prosperous years.

Many famous guests were entertained in the White House during the Coolidge administration. The first was Queen Marie of Romania, for whom a state dinner was given on October 21, 1926. On April 23, 1927, President Machado of Cuba was entertained. By this time, the Coolidges had moved to the Patterson Mansion on Dupont Circle because the White House roof had been found to be dangerous and repairs were necessary.

The most famous guest entertained during the Coolidge administration was Charles Lindbergh, who came to Washington on June 10, 1927, after completing his triumphant solo flight to Paris.

Early in the Coolidge administration, another Prince of Wales visited Washington. The young Prince was invited to lunch with the President and Mrs.

Coolidge on August 31, 1924. The luncheon was small and informal, and it was said that for once, Silent Cal was forced, because of the shyness of the Prince, to carry the conversation with his First Lady throughout the entire meal. The Prince was described as "ill at ease."

There was no representation of Coolidge china at the White House until Mrs. Eisenhower updated and filled in the collection. At that time, April, 1959, John Coolidge, the President's son, donated four plates made by Copeland/Spode. These plates have a wide blue border and are gold-edged. In the center is a laurel wreath tied with a pink bow that encloses a classical urn filled with fruit and foliage. (See Fig. 30.)

Two luncheon plates in the Bachelor's Button pattern, marked "Coronado / H&C / Made in Bohemia," were also given to the collection at this time to represent the Coolidge administration.

The Wilson china was, of course, the official state china used during the Coolidge administration. But a more important remembrance of the era graces the China Room at the White House. The charming full-length portrait, by Howard Chandler Christy, of Grace Coolidge with her dog, Rob Roy, is the only painting hanging in the China Room.

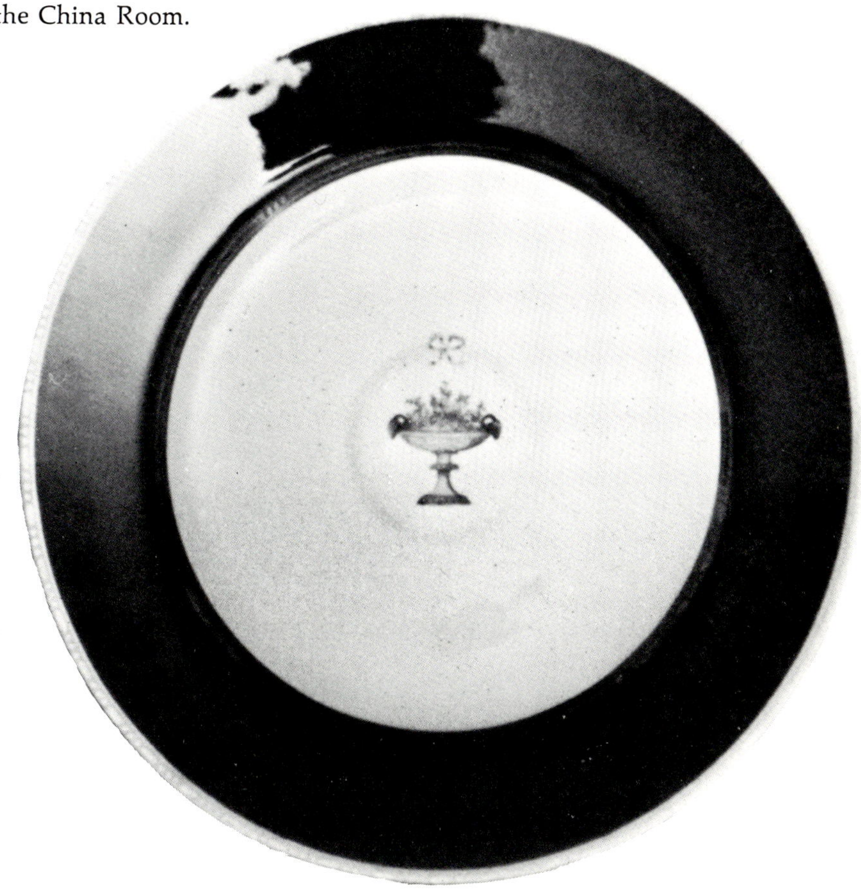

Fig. 30 Plate representing the Coolidge administration in White House china collection. Spode. Border is deep blue with a gold edge. Gold laurel wreath is tied with pink bow.

CHAPTER 31

Herbert Clark Hoover
1929–1933

It was said of Mrs. Hoover that she brought back to the White House the twenty-four wagonloads of clutter that Chester Arthur had had cleaned out. The truth is that Mrs. Hoover did have a desire to return historic artifacts to the White House. She had the White House records studied and began a project in research which, had it been continued, would have led to a mansion authentically furnished, with carefully catalogued objects.

A special project of Mrs. Hoover's was the restoration of the Monroe sitting room. She collected all the authentic Monroe furniture and had reproduction pieces made in the same style. This room was dismantled during the Franklin Roosevelt administration, but was subsequently replaced.

In spite of the sad state of the economy during the Hoover administration, the President and First Lady entertained in an elegant style. Guests were present at almost every meal. The meals were all served in a very formal manner, and on the rare occasions when the Hoovers dined alone, they used the State Dining Room.

Unlike the Coolidges, the Hoovers did not economize in their entertaining, and larger crowds than ever were invited to the frequent White House entertainments. The best of everything was served, and out-of-season food was the rule rather than the exception. However, the Hoovers could not have been entirely unaware of the economic crisis taking place outside of the Executive Mansion. Extra Secret Service guards were added to the existing force to stand duty in the family quarters at night. Lillian Rogers Parks, a White House maid during the Hoover administration, said that Mrs. Hoover, although a kind and considerate woman, was so busy concentrating on making each party the finest, that she did not see the worried faces of the staff, who were losing their savings while the banks went under.

The Hoovers breakfasted in the China Room and undoubtedly appreciated the collection that had been gathered by previous First Ladies. Although the state china used during the Hoover administration was the Lenox service ordered by President Wilson, it is obvious that this one set of china would not have sufficed for such a great amount of entertaining. When Mrs. Eisenhower completed the collection during her husband's administration, Herbert Hoover sent

Fig. 31 Wedgwood plate in Edme shape, with blue and gold decoration, was owned by Herbert Hoover.

samples of other formal dinner services used during his administration. One group is Wedgwood, purchased through Plummer's in New York. A dinner plate, a luncheon plate, and a bread-and-butter plate from this service were donated. The decoration is of gold bell flowers around a white border with gold edging. Gold laurel leaves encircle the large mottled blue center. Another Hoover china pattern is Copenhagen, with a blue on white pattern with a central flower and vine design and a sunburst border. Three plates from this service were also sent to the White House by President Hoover. (See Figs. 31, 32.)

Fig. 32 Plate with blue decoration and swirl border, the Copenhagen pattern, was sent to Mrs. Eisenhower by Herbert Hoover to represent his administration in the White House China Room. The state china used was, of course, the Wilson Lenox.

CHAPTER 32

Franklin Delano Roosevelt
1933–1945

The Roosevelt administration brought life and vigor to the White House and hope to a troubled citizenry. Along with the Roosevelts, their children, and grandchildren, came Mrs. Henrietta Nesbitt, brought to the White House from Hyde Park to serve as housekeeper. In spite of the millions of words written by and about the Franklin Roosevelts, it is to Mrs. Nesbitt's records that we may look for information concerning the Roosevelt style of entertaining and the Presidential china of that administration.

To the active Roosevelts, plates would hardly be an item worthy of much mention. Too many other important things occupied their time and attention. Informal family dinners and many ceremonious state dinners as well as numerous luncheons and teas were held throughout the long Roosevelt administration. The White House was seldom without semipermanent houseguests during this period of American history.

Many illustrious guests were entertained at the White House during the Roosevelt years. Among them were Winston Churchill, King George II of Greece, Madame Chiang Kai-shek, King Peter of Yugoslavia, and Queen Wilhelmina of the Netherlands. However, the most important Royal visitors to the White

House were King George VI and Queen Elizabeth of England. This visit took place on June 8 and 9, 1939, after which the royal party spent the weekend with the Roosevelts at Hyde Park. This marked the first time that a reigning British monarch had paid an official visit to the United States, and a great many preparations took place to ready the White House for the occasion.

Mrs. Nesbitt recorded that although Mrs. Woodrow Wilson had started the Lenox service when she was First Lady, conditions had changed since then and the White House needed more plates. Evidently, a large number of the Wilson plates had been broken by this time.

The Roosevelt state china, also made by Lenox, was designed in part by Franklin Roosevelt. It has a cobalt blue border with an inner gold border of feathers and roses taken from the Roosevelt family crest. The President's seal, with the eagle looking to the left, is in the center of each service plate.

It is probable, too, that along with the Lenox china, new Wedgwood plates were ordered. Mrs. Nesbitt describes the table in the state dining room, set for King George and Queen Elizabeth's visit, as looking beautiful, "with the gold Monroe plate and the new crested glasses, the new Lenox and Wedgwood pieces." There seems to be no record of these "Wedgwood pieces" either at the White House or at Hyde Park, but the ordering of such plates from England might have been a courtesy to the British monarchs on the part of the Roosevelts. Historically, from the time that Woodrow Wilson ordered the first American-made state dinner service, the purchase of foreign-made pottery or porcelain for the White House has never been publicized. In 1939, the slogan "Buy American" had too much importance for a purchase of British china to have been announced.

It is probably for patriotic reasons that the Roosevelt Lenox is spoken of as the only china used at the White House during that long administration. But it is unlikely that this is fact. At Hyde Park, in addition to many commemorative plates presented to the Roosevelts, are two serving pieces from a Haviland set donated by Mrs. James A. Halsted (Anna Roosevelt). Both the tureen and the platter appear to have had rather hard use over the years. They are white Haviland with a blue edge and bear the monogram "F. D. R." The legend on the undersides of these dishes explains their origin. Written in gold is: "Au President

/ Franklin Delano Roosevelt / Un Bon Artisan de la Paix / Septembre 1938 / Theodore Haviland / Limoges / France." These two dishes were part of a service presented to President Roosevelt by the Union Fédérale des Mutils Combattants du Limousin as an expression of gratitude for his persistent efforts in the maintenance of peace.

There seems to be some controversy surrounding a set of china that was owned by the Roosevelts while they occupied the White House. Although there seems to be little doubt that this china was in the White House, since a box of the plates is still in storage there, a member of the curatorial staff seemed to feel that the china had not been used. Several pieces of this service are owned by Hyde Park, also. The service plates are marked "Lenox," but the remainder of the pieces are marked "Theodore Haviland / New York / Made in America."

Fig. 33 Mark on reverse of Roosevelt china. *(Private collection. Photograph by Charles Klamkin.)*

The Lenox service plates are white with a wide cream border decorated with rather large gold stars. On each service plate is a reproduction of the obverse of the Great Seal of the United States in gold. The somewhat stylized eagle is designed in an Art Deco manner popular in the thirties and somewhat resembles the NRA eagle. The Haviland pieces do not have the star or eagle motifs. Although no proof seems to be available, it is probable that these plates were purchased for use at the New York World's Fair during the visit of the King and Queen of England. Luncheon was served to the royal visitors in the Federal Building at the fair on Saturday, June 10, 1939. Such an event would require plates of good quality, and it is probable that this occasion was the only one on which the "World's Fair plates" were used. It is possible also that two manufacturers were needed to produce the required amount of plates in the limited time available.

Henrietta Nesbitt told of the great amount of pilferage of household articles belonging to the White House during the Roosevelt administration. Souvenir seekers have always been a problem at the White House. Mrs. Nesbitt said that silver, dishes, and linens were watched, but that things vanished just the same. The practice of monogramming table linens and silver was stopped by Mrs. Nesbitt in an effort to discourage the theft of these objects. Replacement during wartime was costly and difficult. The help, according to Mrs. Nesbitt, were far more trustworthy than the guests.

Little was done to improve the appearance and structure of the White House during the Roosevelt years. Eleanor Roosevelt was far more interested in improving the working conditions of the White House staff than she was in redecoration. But she renovated and modernized the White House kitchen, which was extremely antiquated. Mrs. Hoover had refused to cross the threshold into the kitchen area while she lived at the White House, but it was one of the first rooms Eleanor Roosevelt asked to see when she toured the mansion that was to become her home for so many years. (See Fig. 33, Plate 26.)

CHAPTER 33

Harry S Truman
1945–1953

Many First Ladies, no matter how unpretentious their beginnings, acted as though an invisible cloak of royalty were placed upon them as soon as they entered the White House. Others, overpowered by the position they found themselves in through their husbands' political ambitions, simply withdrew. Bess Truman was, perhaps, the one First Lady who was the least awed and the least changed by her position as official hostess of the White House. Following the death of Franklin Roosevelt, the Truman family simply changed residences and continued as best as possible under the circumstances to lead the same family life they had always led.

Closely knit and protective of each other in circumstances that are hardly conducive to privacy, the Trumans were popular with the White House staff and, as it turned out in the election of 1948, with enough members of the general public. The plain, unassuming Bess Truman, unhappy in the public eye, was well liked. Her honest image as a wife, mother, and housekeeper appealed to the American people.

The first term of the Truman administration was of historical importance in White House history. It is possible that only a seasoned politician like Harry

Truman could have convinced Congress that the White House was in danger of collapsing and needed complete rebuilding. While the painstaking work of gutting the building, marking each bit of paneling and stone for replacement, and removing the old materials to a storage area was taking place, the Trumans moved across the street to Blair House. During this period, the adjoining Lee House became guest quarters for visitors to the First Family. Official entertainments were carried on at a Washington hotel. However, when Princess Elizabeth and the Duke of Edinburgh visited the Trumans in the fall of 1951, a dinner was held for them at Blair House.

The renovated White House became home again for the Trumans before the end of Harry Truman's administration. Although an entirely new structure inside, the only Truman mark on the exterior was the balcony that was to be enjoyed by subsequent First Families. Other niceties, such as air conditioning and ceilings and floors that were not in danger of collapsing, are also attributed to this peppery President.

For the new house, President and Mrs. Truman also ordered a new dinner service from Lenox. For this service President Truman standardized the Presidential seal that adorns the plates by turning the eagle's head in the direction of the olive branches instead of the arrows. Another departure on the Truman china are the colors used in the decoration. Where most state china with patriotic motifs had featured a blue or red border, the Truman china has borders of teal green and pale yellow. A wide embossed-gold outer rim and a narrow inner rim of gold decorate the service plates of the Truman china, and the President's seal, surrounded by gold stars, is the central theme. The same motif, in a smaller version, is placed on the rim of the dinner plates. (See Plate 26.)

CHAPTER 34

Dwight David Eisenhower
1953–1961

The White House, a temporary home for all its residents, was the house the Eisenhowers occupied for a longer period than any other residence. As the wife of a career army man, Mamie Doud Eisenhower could easily make the adjustment of moving. A warm and friendly person, she was used to making friends in new locations, although she was hardly a stranger to Washington by the time her husband became President of the United States.

Any army wife soon learns that she must be adaptable to new houses and new locations, and Mrs. Eisenhower made these changes perhaps with a better will than most. Packing up and moving on became a way of life for her, and since the houses and apartments she lived in could not be hers, she learned early in her marriage the value of continuity in the furniture and decorative objects that she moved from place to place. She overcame homesickness in strange surroundings by having her rooms painted in the same colors and by placing her own bric-a-brac about so that each new address took on a familiarity. Her favorite colors, pink and green, meant "home" to her and were used in the First Family's living quarters in the White House during her husband's administration.

Mamie Eisenhower has a keen interest in ceramics, which she put to good use in her work on the china collection while she occupied the White House. She had the Presidential china rearranged in chronological order. This was the obvious way for the china relics to be displayed, but it had not previously been done. While at work on this project, Mrs. Eisenhower discovered that there were five administrations that were not represented in the china collection; and she, along with her secretary, Mrs. McCaffree, and a member of the curatorial staff of the Smithsonian Institution, contacted the heirs of the five former Presidents and completed the collection. The five administrations not represented were those of Presidents Andrew Johnson, William Howard Taft, Warren G. Harding, Calvin Coolidge, and Herbert Hoover. A cup and saucer were obtained from the Harding Museum in Ohio; two Wedgwood plates were sent to represent the Hoover administration; four Spode plates were given to represent the administration of Calvin Coolidge; three different china relics that had been used by President Taft were added; and a sugar bowl that had been the property of Andrew Johnson completed the china collection.

Mrs. Eisenhower, in answer to the author's inquiry concerning the china used at the White House while she was First Lady, stated, "There was a great deal of the Roosevelt and Truman china left, so that it was not necessary for us to buy a complete service.

"As to the service plates that General Eisenhower and I chose, we took a very small concern that we never had china represented in the White House. I was most interested in giving this gentleman (whose name I have forgotten) the opportunity to make these service plates."

The service plates of which Mrs. Eisenhower speaks were made by Castleton. They are a light cream color with the Presidential seal in the center and a four-inch border in heavy gold. The 120 plates were selected in 1955, and the plate rim, of coin gold, has a raised medallion design. Eight separate firings were required to achieve the desired finish. The Eisenhower service plates are, perhaps, the most elegant of all White House china and a fitting representation of one of the few First Ladies in this century who realized the historical value of a continuing display of Presidential china in the White House. (See Plate 4.)

Mamie Eisenhower collected her family china while traveling with her husband to many posts in the world. Most of the Eisenhower family china is Minton from England, although Mrs. Eisenhower wrote that she owns a couple of fine sets of Japanese porcelain.

Of great historical interest is the Eisenhower personal dinner set of Rosenthal china, a complete service that has the general's insignia of a flaming sword as decoration. Mrs. Eisenhower wrote that because there was no gold available at the time, the gold that was used on these plates was from some gold pieces General Eisenhower carried on his person. He gave these to the Rosenthal people, and they placed it on the china. She said, "This, of course, will go to David as he was named for his grandfather."

Two relics that are associated with the Presidential china at the White House are a part of the national collection thanks to Mrs. Eisenhower's efforts. An

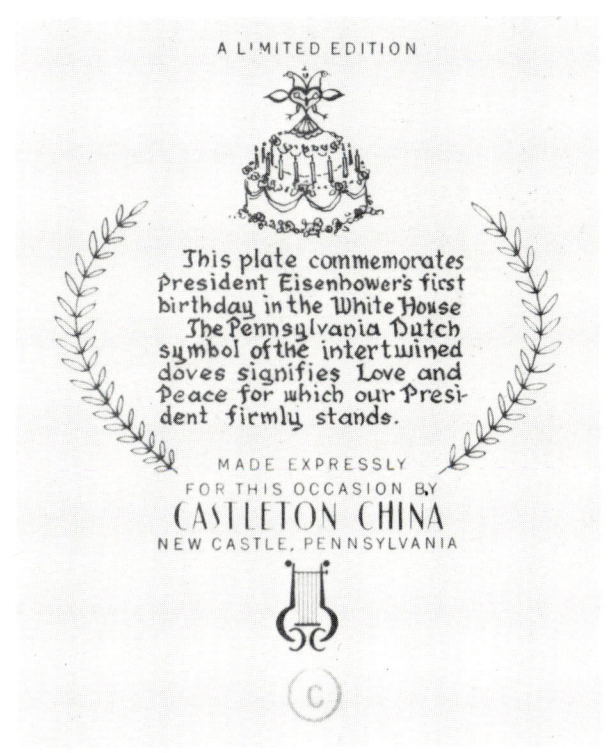

Fig. 34 Legend on reverse of Eisenhower birthday plate.
(Private collection. Photograph by Charles Klamkin.)

original engraving of a Theodore Davis design used in the production of the large turkey platter of the Hayes dinner service made by Haviland in 1879 was presented to the White House china collection during the Eisenhower administration. Another relic of interest is a painting of *A White House Orchid* by Mrs. Benjamin Harrison. This historic picture was presented to Mrs. Eisenhower for the White House China Room in December, 1958. Neither of these objects is currently on display in the China Room.

During her years in the White House, Mamie Eisenhower was a gracious hostess who entertained on a somewhat smaller scale than previous First Ladies. The Eisenhowers were less formal in their entertainments, and the First Lady sometimes used imagination and humor in her decorations. One party, for the wives of White House staff members, featured Halloween decorations in the stately State Dining Room. Skeletons and witches on broomsticks, as well as ears of corn and other fall decorations, were used. Dinners and luncheons for the many foreign dignitaries who visited the White House during the Eisenhower years were, of course, held in a more formal atmosphere.

Although a more private person than many First Ladies, Mamie Doud Eisenhower left a more permanent mark than many in the work she accomplished in the China Room on the ground floor of the White House. (See Fig. 34, Plate 26.)

CHAPTER 35

John Fitzgerald Kennedy
1961–1963

During the Kennedy administration, many changes took place in the formality of White House entertaining. Mrs. Kennedy personalized the White House parties just as she personalized the White House itself. A lady of elegance, beauty, and superb taste, Jacqueline Bouvier Kennedy was a conscientious hostess who gave as much attention to her cuisine as she did to her guests' comfort and pleasure.

More than any previous First Lady, Mrs. Kennedy felt the importance of the history of the mansion she and her young family occupied, and she was instrumental in restoring to the White House, through gifts and purchases, many of the decorative objects of historical importance. Perhaps her greatest accomplishment along these lines was her effort in having a law passed so that future Presidential families could not sell or throw out objects that were a part of the White House collection.

Old traditions were done away with in an effort to make the White House a warm and happy place to visit. The Kennedy guests were entertained in a relaxed atmosphere, and the White House came alive with bright bouquets of flowers, good food and conversation, and superb after-dinner entertainment.

The dinner service of the Truman administration, with its yellow and green borders, was set off by pale yellow table linens, which were used on the innovative small tables that Mrs. Kennedy preferred to the long banquet table previously used. Smaller tables and careful grouping of guests led to more interesting dinner conversation and an informal atmosphere. Cocktails before dinner and fewer courses of food, superbly prepared, also added to the success of Kennedy dinners.

Mrs. Kennedy used the historic china of previous administrations as often as possible, and photographs of table settings at the White House during the Kennedy administration show that the Harrison, Lincoln, and Roosevelt services were used. It is obvious that Mrs. Kennedy was aware of the history of many of the sets of Presidential china, and she was instrumental in obtaining a plate from the Monroe dessert service for the China Room and the Smithsonian Institution.

There are no plates that represent the Kennedy administration in the China Room at the White House. The Kennedy glassware ordered for the White House from West Virginia, the china previously purchased by President Harry Truman, and the Eisenhower service plates, as well as the china already mentioned, were used throughout the Kennedy years. However, photographs of the Kennedys' dining room in their Georgetown residence taken before the inauguration reveal a Wedgwood Queen's ware tureen and platter that were used on a side table. These classic eighteenth-century pieces represent Mrs. Kennedy's taste and interest in objects that were the best of their period. "The best" of American taste is the quality that Mrs. Kennedy hoped to bring to the White House, and in the short time she lived there, she succeeded. (See Plate 27.)

CHAPTER 36

Lyndon Baines Johnson
1963–1969

Mrs. Lyndon Johnson, our first First Lady from Texas, came to the White House with an awareness of the historical importance of both the happenings and the objects connected with the mansion. Her dedicated interest in the beautiful and the historical shows up on every page of her book *A White House Diary*, the most complete record ever kept of one Presidential administration by a First Lady.

Throughout Lady Bird Johnson's book are references to the historical collection of White House china. She speaks of using the plates that remained of the various dinner services of previous administrations. One luncheon, to which members of a group interested in historic preservation had been invited, featured each small table set with china of a different provenance. The Lincoln china, the Hayes china, the Harrison china, a Thomas Jefferson tureen, and the Theodore Roosevelt Wedgwood were used. One table featured Mrs. Johnson's own dinner service.

Mrs. Johnson gave a great deal of thought and effort to choosing a pattern for the Johnson dinner service. She describes a meeting with the designers from Tiffany that took place at the White House on Monday, September 25, 1967.

The preliminary work on this design had taken nine months, and the occasion was a meeting for the First Lady's approval of the final pattern. The eagle was patterned after the Monroe eagle, and the design shows that Mrs. Johnson was completely aware of the various motifs used on other White House china and that she wanted the Johnson china to be truly representative of her husband's administration and her personal interests in conservation and beautification.

The previous January, when Mrs. Johnson became aware of the necessity of ordering a complete state dinner service, she went to the China Room of the White House to make a study of the plates on display. She especially liked the Benjamin Harrison china, the Woodrow Wilson set, the Franklin Roosevelt dinner service "with the restrained symbolism of his own coat of arms," the Thomas Jefferson set ("but it is Chinese export"), and the James Monroe set. She recorded at the time that a service done like the Monroe china would be wonderful—"or else it would fall flat on its face!" She admitted it would take a daring First Lady to choose it.

Mrs. Johnson's primary objective in choosing a china pattern was not so much to look for a design that was fashionable or one that simply indicated that the dinner service was made to be used in the President's house, but rather to work out a pattern that would embody the historical meaning of the White House china collection and the personality of the administration for which it would be made. Castleton, in Pennsylvania, was the potter chosen to manufacture the service for Mrs. Johnson.

The Johnson china, the first full dinner service to be ordered for the White House since 1952, was an absolute necessity for the affable Johnsons. A great amount of entertaining took place, and larger groups were invited to the White House more often than ever before. By the time of the first Johnson term of office, the White House china had been depleted, and a service that would suffice for 140 to 190 people was ordered.

The Johnson china was designed by Van Day Truex, with paintings of flowers by Andre Piette, for Tiffany and Company of New York. Mrs. Johnson's interest in the floral beauty of America provided the dominant theme of the Johnson state service. The service plate is bordered in wildflowers with a background of gold dotted vaulting, and a narrow apricot border rims the perimeter. The plate is centered with the figure of an eagle, with wings spread, and a shield taken from the state dessert service of President James Monroe. The dinner plates are similar to the service plates; however, the eagle is reduced in size and appears in the border with wildflowers against the background of the gold dotted vaulting. Each dessert plate is centered with a state flower. (See Plates 27, 28.)

Flowers from all fifty states and the District of Columbia are represented on the Johnson service. The basic decorative design of a radiating pattern of gold dots is carried through the additional pieces. Forty different wild flowers appear on various pieces of the Johnson service. The dinner plates are decorated with the poppy, prickly pear, rain lily, bluebell, eastern dogwood, Indian paintbrush, black-eyed susan, wild white rose, and fluttermill. The service plates feature the bluebonnet, Indian blanket, goldenrod, meadow pink, prairie phlox, bristle-leaved aster, prickly poppy, prairie verbena, evening primrose, and coreopsis. Wine-cup and blue gentian decorate the demitasse cups. (See Plate 4.)

The large and small bowls, made for serving and for flower containers, are decorated with (among others) the crimson clover, scarlet pea, gold star grass, periwinkle, piriqueta, vetchlings, grape hyacinth, desert marigold, wide-leafed spring beauty, desert poppy, tansy aster, blue witch, wild geranium, midland lily, blue-eyed grass, and toothwort.

It should come as no surprise that negotiations, study, research, and design of the Johnson state dinner service took two years, while the production of the china took six months. The unique Johnson dinner service was used for the first time on May 23, 1968, at the annual luncheon traditionally given by the First Lady for the Senate Ladies. In the past, Mrs. Johnson had used the china of the different Presidential administrations for table settings at this luncheon. One hundred guests, including wives of cabinet members and former members of the United States Senate, attended this luncheon. Mrs. Johnson received her guests in the Green Room, and the luncheon was held in the State Dining Room. The Marine band provided background music in the Foyer. Round tables were covered with pale yellow cloths under white organdy covers, and bouquets of spring flowers decorated the tables. The containers for the flower arrangements were small bowls that are a part of the Johnson dinner service.

Although the luncheon marked the first use of the Johnson china, the first public viewing of the unique dinner service took place on May 9, 1968, when Mrs. Johnson gave an afternoon reception in the East Room of the White House. It was announced at this time that the dinner service for 216 place settings included service plates, dinner plates, fish plates, dessert plates, clear and cream soup plates, demitasse cups and saucers, as well as 24 large bowls and 24 smaller bowls suitable for centerpieces for fruit or flowers. On the occasion of the unveiling of the Johnson china, Mrs. Johnson gave a talk in which she explained some of the historical background of the White House china services. She said that the White House china reflects the tastes of past First Ladies—and often of their husbands. She remarked that like the great portraits, the other paintings, and the furniture, the china collection is a cavalcade of the changing personalities and events that have enriched the heritage of the White House. It was obvious that the Johnson china and the various wildflower designs that decorate the plates were a great source of satisfaction and accomplishment to this history-oriented First Lady when she remarked, "The China we are introducing today—is a joy to me."

The Johnson china, said to have cost "under $80,000," "was the gift of an anonymous donor." It is obvious, however, that Lady Bird Johnson was given free choice in the design and decoration of this most recently purchased Presidential china for the White House.

CHAPTER 37

Richard Milhous Nixon
1969–

The Nixon administration brought to the White House a family that covets its privacy as much as many past First Families. It is, perhaps, even more noticeable when one compares the Nixon life-style with that of the outgoing Johnson family.

At the time of this writing, Nixon's third year in office, there seems to be no indication that Mrs. Pat Nixon will choose to purchase new china that will represent her husband's administration in the White House. A statement in the press in 1970 that new Nixon china was being ordered by the First Lady seems to have been either premature or erroneous. Because of the size and completeness of the Johnson china service, there is truly no need for a new state dinner service for the White House.

The most publicized social event held so far during the present administration was the wedding of Tricia Nixon, older daughter of the President, to law student Edward Finch Cox. This White House wedding was held out of doors in the Rose Garden on June 12, 1971. A photograph taken of Miss Nixon; her sister, Mrs. David Eisenhower; and Mrs. Nixon shortly before the wedding day shows the First Lady and her two daughters using the Truman china. However, to this date, the Johnson china is the official state china of the Nixon administration.

CHAPTER 38

Reproductions of Presidential China

From time to time reproductions of Presidential china have been produced, often by the companies that originally made the china, but not always. Sometimes these plates are made to commemorate an event associated with the particular President whom the china pattern represents. The plates most often reproduced are, of course, those that were originally decorated with patriotic motifs.

At no time, in so far as can be ascertained, have any Presidential plates been made for the purpose of being sold as the genuine article. That is, they have never been fraudulently represented as having been the original White House china, but rather as authentic reproductions; and most are specially marked so that there should be no confusion concerning the fact. However, as we have seen with the centennial reproductions made by Haviland, which were marked with the administrations on the reverse sides, collectors believe only what they want to believe, and many of these reproductions have been purchased as original Presidential plates in recent years.

Certainly the plate that has most often been reproduced is the Martha Washington States plate. The original was China trade porcelain in blue, green, and gold on white. A French reproduction of the pattern was made around 1875, probably in anticipation of the centennial celebration. One version of the French reproduction is owned by the Metropolitan Museum in New York (which also owns an original States plate) and is actually a cake plate with handles and a gold rim. Another States plate, probably made at the same time or earlier, is flow-blue with gold and is unmarked. This plate seems to be of Staffordshire manufacture and might have been made to commemorate the centennial of Washington's birth.

Still another fairly recent reproduction of the Martha Washington plate is illustrated here, along with the legend that appears on the reverse side. Made by the Shenango China Company, the quality of this plate and the decoration are

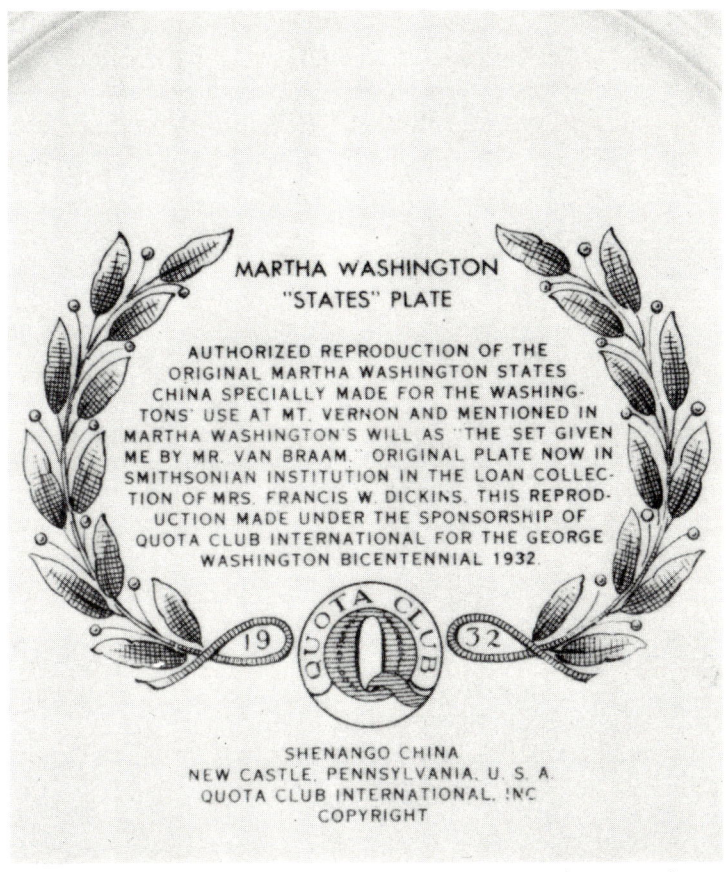

Fig 35   Markings on reverse of Shenango Washington plate. (*Private collection. Photograph by Charles Klamkin.*)

exceptionally good, proving that our American potters are now capable of manufacturing good-quality porcelain. This plate was made for Washington's bicentennial in 1932. (See Fig. 35, Plate 28.)

The centennial celebration in Philadelphia in 1876 seemed to spur the production of a series of Presidential plates that had been made by Haviland-Limoges. The time of the centennial seemed to be propitious for Haviland to reproduce the Lincoln and Grant plates for sale to the public. These plates, honest reproductions not made to fool anyone, are marked on the reverse "Administration Abraham Lincoln" and "Administration U. S. Grant." Since both

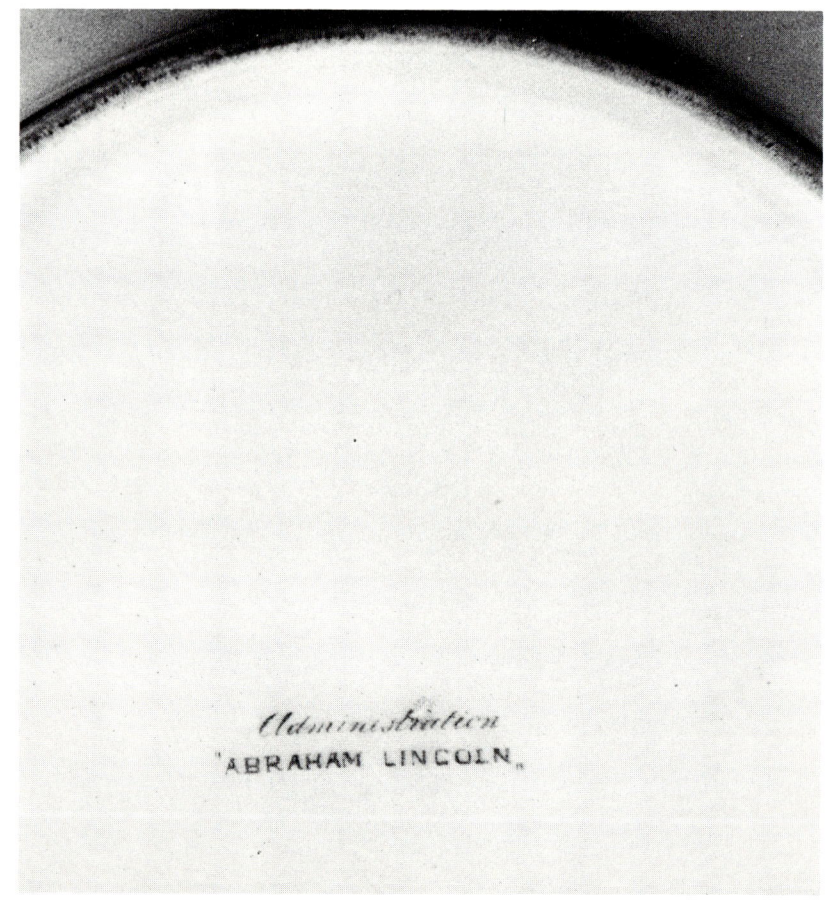

Fig. 36 Centennial reproduction of Lincoln plate had this mark. (*Private collection. Photograph by Charles Klamkin.*)

Fig. 37 Mark on reverse of Grant centennial reproduction. (*Private collection. Photograph by Charles Klamkin.*)

legends are placed within quotation marks, this seems to be further proof that they were not meant to be passed off as the genuine plates of those Presidents. These plates, similar to a series being reproduced almost a hundred years later by Haviland-Limoges, were probably made in limited quantity; and if anything, they are of a somewhat better quality porcelain than the original plates. (See Figs. 36, 37, Plate 1.)

It is obviously not coincidental that Haviland and Company, Limoges, France, began another series of reproductions of Presidential china in 1969, in preparation for the American bicentennial celebration. The first plate released of this series was, however, a reproduction of a Haviland reproduction, even though the series is supposed to represent plates Haviland had designed for the Presidents. This new plate is a reproduction of the Haviland centennial reproduction of the Martha Washington States plate and is 8½ inches in diameter. It was issued in a limited edition of 2,500.

The second plate issued in this series is truly a reproduction of a Haviland pattern. The new Lincoln plate was also issued in a limited edition of 2,500. Each plate is numbered, signed by Theodore Haviland II, and bears the legend, "Authentic reproduction of a plate made by Haviland at Limoges, France, in 1861 for President Abraham Lincoln and personally selected by Mary Todd Lincoln." Lincoln plate number 1 was presented to President Nixon, while numbers 2 and 3 were placed on display in the White House and the Smithsonian Institution.

A third plate in this series is a reproduction of one of the Grant plates that has a center design of a rose. Other plates in the series, which are being brought out at the rate of one edition per year, are a Hayes plate, an Andrew Johnson plate, a Franklin Pierce plate (we assume with a red border), a James Garfield plate, (*not* state china), and one that belonged to Chester A. Arthur. Interestingly, the Smithsonian Institution has loaned its name to the project, and a member of the Smithsonian's staff is authenticating each plate as having been made by Haviland and Company, a fact no one would dispute in any case.

Haviland-Limoges seems to have a history of being able to reproduce Presidential china services almost simultaneously with the delivery to the administration for which the original was made. Such was the case with the Hayes china. The condition on which President Hayes was able to have such elaborate china made for a comparatively low price seems to have been that Haviland would be allowed to make and sell comparable sets of the same design.

Although Wedgwood has continually made the Colonnade pattern in bone china that was designed for Theodore Roosevelt, it has never been reproduced with the obverse of the Presidential seal in the border, except on White House order.

Unless one considers later orders for White House china that were made to fill in incomplete services of previous administrations, there seem to be no reproductions aside from those mentioned above. It is highly probable that other potteries besides Haviland will soon begin to reproduce patterns that have been used in the White House for the American bicentennial celebration. As interest in our own heritage grows, so will the collectors' interest in the china used by our Presidents and their First Ladies. For those collectors who already possess examples of Presidential china, every new issue of a reproduction is an interesting event.

Many private collectors of White House china have long had an interest in the preservation of White House historical objects, and their collections are only a part of their efforts to foster this interest in others. It is fortunate that the residents of the White House themselves have lately shown a desire to preserve what is left of the artifacts that are representative of previous administrations. Had the preceding administrations (before the Kennedy years) had an interest in preserving historical objects of the White House, Presidential china would not have come into the hands of the private collectors, who, fortunately, have preserved it so carefully.

As the country approaches its two hundredth anniversary, a new look at our own sense of history and the relics that represent it is advisable. The White House collection of Presidential china is one that will grow continually. It is to be hoped that many of the interesting objects of historical value that were sent out of the White House as "junk" will find their way back some day. It would also be desirable for the only continuing collection of Presidential objects in the country to be placed on view for all Americans to look at.

CHAPTER 39

Auctions of Private Collections of Presidential China

It may come as a surprise to many that White House china can be found in numerous private collections in America. However, once one is aware of the policy of the dispersal of White House furnishings that existed well into this century, one can only be amazed that the White House collection exists at all.

In an article written for *Munsey's Magazine,* in December, 1903, Abby Gunn Baker discussed the methods used to dispose of damaged china. She said:

> In the early history of the republic Congress twice a year appointed a committee from its own numbers to visit the White House, look through its cupboards and closets and receive the steward's report of breakages. In this way it was supposed that the china and plate would be kept intact; but the solemn inspection of the Congressional Solons was no safeguard against wear and tear, nor could it prevent the duplicity of servants who were willing, for a consideration, to transfer specimens to the cabinets of unscrupulous private collectors.
>
> A nick, crack or blemish has always been a sufficient cause for discarding china from the President's table. Formerly the damaged ware was kept through each administration until with the incoming of a new mistress it was sold to the second-hand dealers of Washington. It was in this way that much of the Presidential china has reached private collectors.

Mrs. Baker neglected to mention one other method of getting rid of the damaged china. It was not unusual for auctions of unwanted White House furnishings to be held. Many White House plates were purchased in this manner. The largest auction held was during Chester Arthur's administration, when twenty-four wagonloads of goods were cleaned out of the White House and sent to Duncanson Brothers, Auctioneers. It has been said that William Crump, a member of the White House staff from May, 1879, to May, 1882, purchased over three hundred pieces of china during that sale. A great many pieces of Presidential china in private collections can be traced directly to the Crump collection.

Mrs. Baker also recorded that a large lot of china "that was more or less injured, but which was invaluable in that it could not be replaced, was gathered up in 1893 [Grover Cleveland's administration] and sold in a lot to second-hand dealers." It was not long after this that Mrs. Baker began her study of the china in the White House, and subsequent articles written by her obviously created a demand for the china by private collectors. She cites the fact that Colonel Crook (another White House employee) bought a cracked Lincoln pitcher in 1893 for $2.50 and that "plates bearing the historic seal, on which the gilt had dimmed, or which showed a crack or nick, sold for a dollar each." Mrs. Baker said that if a similar sale were to take place during the year she wrote the article, 1903, "such things would bring fabulous prices."

The earliest record of an auction of ceramics from a private collection that included examples of Presidential china is a printed catalogue of the *"Governor Caleb Lyon Collections of Oriental and Occidental Ceramics."* This sale was held after the death of Governor Lyon, and the collection at the time was the property of his daughter-in-law, Mrs. H. D. Lyon. The sale took place at the auction gallery of Henry D. Miner, 845 Broadway, New York, on Monday, April 24, 1876. The collection, which included many Oriental works of ceramic art as well as fine English and French pottery and porcelain, was the lifetime collection of Governor Lyon, who had traveled abroad and had become aware of the European craze for porcelain collecting. Few Americans had any interest in amassing collections of ceramics in the mid-nineteenth century. (See Fig. 38.)

In the introduction to the Lyon auction catalogue it is stated that "the collection now offered for sale is the result of a life-work, commenced before the taste for forming cabinets had been inaugurated in America save by a few, but when the passion in Europe was in its Zenith."

Thirty pieces of Presidential china, said to represent Presidents Grant, Lincoln, Pierce, Taylor, Van Buren, John Quincy Adams, Monroe, Madison, Jefferson, John Adams, and Washington, were auctioned in the Lyon sale. The catalogue is of importance because many attributions of Presidential china have been made from the descriptions of the various pieces included in it. However, Governor Lyon was obviously as confused as many collectors and curators have been about some of the attributions. A plate described as "Taylor," number 836, "A round gilt-edged Plate of French porcelain with a dark red rim broken by coffee-colored compartments filled with the implements and symbols of agriculture, commerce, science, and arts. The white centre is decorated with the American Eagle flying through space, the shield and motto of the United States around his neck" is now attributed to the Monroe administration. The plate, by the way, had five compartments in the border, the last representing strength or warfare.

The most realistic attributions in the Governor Lyon catalogue are listings of ceramics presented directly to the collector by Presidents who were his contemporaries. A Grant plate, number 823, is described as "a lovely scolloped edged Plate of French porcelain with a dark cream-colored band around the rim; broken by a medallion, enclosing the American Eagle with motto, surmounted by thirteen stars, exquisitely executed in red and gold; in the centre a large bouquet of finely painted flowers." Another plate and a coffee cup and saucer from the same set were also sold.

Another group of French china, presented by President Lincoln to Governor Lyon in 1865, included number 826: "An irregular gilt-edged French porcelain Plate with rim decorated in dark purple and gold. In the centre the spread-eagle, against a golden sky, rests upon the American shield, which is upheld by a ribbon inscribed with the National motto, floating in clouds. Finely painted." Two plates from the Lincoln service were sold. The records show that two egg cups from the same service were purchased at the Lyon auction by P. A. Wolcott of Orange, New Jersey, who noted that he sold one cup "for a *large price* to a

HENRY D. MINER, - Auctioneer,
Late Henry H. Leeds & Miner. Established 1847.

CATALOGUE

OF THE

"Governor Caleb Lyon

COLLECTION OF

ORIENTAL

AND

OCCIDENTAL CERAMICS,"

BELONGING TO MRS. H. D. LYON,

TO BE SOLD AT AUCTION,

By HENRY D. MINER, Auctioneer,

COMMENCING

Monday, April 24th, 1876,

At 11 o'clock A. M.,

AND THE FOLLOWING DAYS,

At his Art Galleries, 845 Broadway.

NOW ON EXHIBITION FREE.

TERMS OF SALE—CASH.

A deposit required from all purchasers, at the option of the Auctioneer. Purchases to be paid for and removed within 24 hours or deposits forfeited, or said purchases to be resold for account of purchaser, at Auctioneer's option.

John Polhemus, Printer, 102 Nassau Street.

Fig. 38 Earliest known and recorded auction of private collection of Presidential china had many erroneous attributions. Later labels in White House collection seem to have been taken from the Lyon catalogue. (*Private collection. Photograph by Charles Klamkin.*)

collector in 1878 and in 1880 was offered more than double the price" for the other.

Number 835, described in the catalogue, as having belonged to President Pierce, is "a circular gilt-edge Plate of French porcelain rimmed with a coffee-colored band and gilt ring in the centre." This is probably the Lincoln buff-edged china.

Numbers 838 and 839 were described as "curiously shaped" plates, neither round nor square, "of French porcelain with scroll-work in bas relief on rim. The decoration consists of gilt sparingly used, and the shield and motto of the United States in color." Obviously this is the Polk china.

To President Jackson was attributed number 840: "A plate of the same shape as the preceding, with the shield, but having an apple-green rim and a group of finely painted flowers in the centre." This was not one of Jackson's plates, but rather another of the Polk service.

An interesting attribution is that applied to numbers 842 and 843. These are listed as having once belonged to President John Quincy Adams and are described as "an exquisite irregular-edged Plate with a simple decoration of blue-and-gold bands, a shield ornaments the centre. French porcelain." These plates, even with the meager description, can be none other than the controversial dessert service attributed at various times to both Jackson and Madison, but which in reality could not have been made before the time of President Pierce and is more likely Buchanan. (See Chapter 16.)

To President Madison are attributed numbers 847, 848, and 849. These items include a coffee cup and saucer decorated with gold bands and the initial "M": "A white and gilt plate with simple but curious ornamentation in pink panels; on the rim are sea monsters in white sailing from each other, and a plate with cream colored rim decorated with gold."

"A splendid plate of Chinese manufacture with rim and inner border diapered in dark blue relieved by gold tracery. In the centre the letter 'J' in gold is enclosed in a shield, the outline of which is of blue enamel adorned by the thirteen stars. A helmet with visor closed, in light blue, surmounts the shield" is said to have belonged to President Jefferson. "A custard stand of French porcelain decorated with detached bachelor's buttons" is also said to have been

President Jefferson's; this latter pattern has been attributed to various Presidents of the early part of the nineteenth century.

President John Adams is said to have used numbers 852, 853, and 854. The first item is described as "an octagonal Chinese plate with basketwork rim and

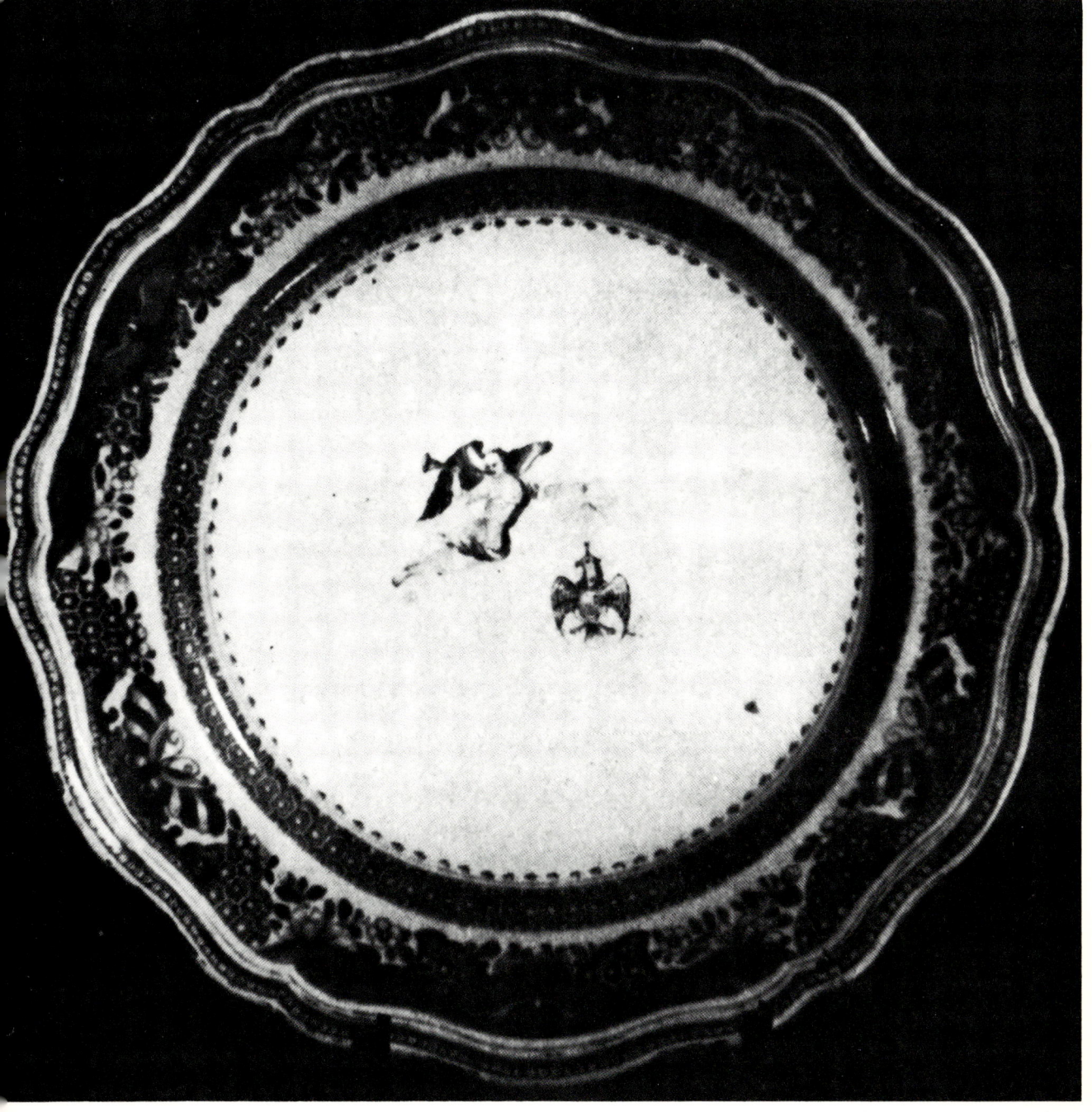

Fig. 39 Washington Cincinnati plate with flaw in porcelain (at four o'clock) was simple to trace through catalogues of several auctions. (*From Auction Catalogue: Part 2 of the Collection of the late Frances Clemson Cross. Photograph by Charles Klamkin.*)

blue diapered inner border; the willow pattern on the center." Number 853 is identical, and the last is "another [plate] of French porcelain decorated in blue and gold."

The attributions to President Washington in the Governor Lyon auction catalogue are the "white, scolloped-edged, Sèvres Porcelain Plate; the only decoration consists of a narrow gold bordering around the edge." A further note explains "to understand the importance attached to such a simple ornamentation, one must recollect that at this time all the factories in the kingdom were forbidden to gild their porcelain, excepting the royal manufactory at Sèvres; it is to be regretted that this invaluable piece is imperfect, as a small fragment has been broken from the rim."

Number 856 is also a Washington plate and is described as "a Plate of the immortal 'Cincinnati China' presented by the French officers to their late Commander-in-Chief." A second plate from the same service and "A Plate from a set presented to Mrs. Washington at the same time; with monogram 'M. W.' a gilt star in the centre" were also auctioned.

The information for the Lyon catalogue was probably taken from the governor's own writings. At the time of his death, he was compiling a book including examples of porcelain from his and others' collections.

In May, 1895, an issue of *China, Glass and Lamps*, a trade journal, printed a short article entitled "George Washington's China Sold." It stated that

> The Philadelphia Press of May 10, (1895) says of an auction sale in that city: Some chinaware presented to George Washington attracted the attention of bidders. A Cincinnati Nankin china dinner plate, decorated with gold bands and a blue margin at the Royal factory at Sèvres, with the insignia of the Society of the Cincinnati, brought $130. This is a piece of a set presented to General Washington by the French officers of the society. Auctioneer Henkels also offered for a sale a magnificent collection of five pieces of chinaware presented to General Washington by French officers of the society, but no person cared to bid high enough for the curios. The auctioneer said that they had been sold previously for $1200. The pieces are ornamented with gold bands and a blue margin and were decorated at the Royal factory at Sèvres. . . . Later these pieces were offered for sale and were bought by Dr. Copp for $600.

From time to time in this century, plates claimed to have been used in the White House have been offered for sale at auction. Most of these plates are from well-recognized services of Presidential china such as the Grant set, the Polk set, and most often, the Hayes dinner service. Quite frequently these are reproductions. At least a dozen or more complete services of the Hayes pattern were produced by Haviland, and other Haviland patterns of White House china were reproduced during the centennial and the Columbian exposition.

Perhaps the most highly publicized auctions of Presidential china of this century took place in two separate sessions at the Parke-Bernet Galleries in New York. The dates of the first session were April 30 and May 1, 1954. The auction consisted of *Select Early American Furniture and Silver, American Historical China, Paintings, Glass & Other Property from the Collection of Stanley S. Wohl, Annapolis, Md. and from other owners.*

The most important item of interest to historians of the George Washington era was a Washington "Historic Oriental Lowestoft Blue and White Plate Decorated with the Order of the Cincinnati." An additional note in the catalogue says, "this plate comes from the famous service brought over from China by Capt. Samuel Shaw of Boston, first Secretary of the Order of the Cincinnati, in 1785, and presented by him to George Washington." The plate brought $1,550 at this auction. It has, as we will note later, increased enormously in value since that time.

The next listing in the Wohl auction of Presidential china is a "Porcelain breakfast cup and saucer, valanced blue and gold edge enclosing a banding of scattered gilded pellets centring a cartouche, the interior with a deep gilded band." The catalogue description calls the cup and saucer "a unique item, and probably the only existing example in private hands. This historic cup and saucer, in addition to a plate and teacup and saucer (now in the china room of the White House) and the Stuart portrait of Washington in the East Room, are believed to be the only furnishings of the White House to survive the burning by the British in 1814." Obviously, these are the same cup and saucer of Haviland-Limoges origin that could not possibly have belonged to Dolley Madison but that are now considered to have been purchased by James Buchanan.

The "Madison" cup and saucer sold for $575, an amount that obviously would not have been reached were they not given this romantic provenance.

To James Monroe the Wohl catalogue attributes the buff-bordered china that belonged to Mrs. Lincoln. Item number 278 is described in the catalogue as "a porcelain Boat Stand bordered in buff with narrow gildings." The source given for identification is an article written by Theodore Davis in the *Ladies Home Journal*, May, 1889. Mr. Davis's article is not too accurate, either, so both Parke-Bernet and Mr. Wohl are to be forgiven.

None of the other pieces of Presidential china of this first session of the Wohl auction at Parke-Bernet brought such staggering prices as the Cincinnati plate and the so-called Madison cup and saucer. A red-bordered Pierce tea plate and olive dish sold for $40, an Abraham Lincoln dessert plate (in truth, a centennial reproduction bearing the legend "Administration / Abraham Lincoln" on the back) brought $190; and another [Lincoln dessert plate], damaged, brought $90. A U. S. Grant porcelain dessert plate, also a centennial reproduction made by Haviland, but described incorrectly as being an authentic Grant plate, brought $130; and a Hayes dinner plate "decorated with a night setting of a wolf seated beside a lake and howling at the moon, a forest fire in the distance," sold for $60. Three Benjamin Harrison dessert plates brought $100 each. Mrs. William McKinley's porcelain cup and saucer, decorated with wide borders of pink roses between royal blue and gold floral bandings, and also made by Haviland-Limoges, brought $120 at the first Wohl sale.

A second group of Presidential china from the Wohl collection was auctioned at Parke-Bernet Galleries on Saturday afternoon, March 26, 1955. The first item auctioned in the group was a "James Madison Porcelain Dinner Plate" that matched the cup and saucer sold at the earlier Wohl auction. Since the cup and saucer had been described as "a unique item, and probably the only existing example in private hands," it is interesting that in the course of a year, Mr. Wohl somehow managed to find another piece of this service. This time the plate brought only $225; however, this was a considerable amount compared with some of the low prices other pieces of Presidential china brought on that day.

Number 280, a porcelain tea plate attributed to Franklin Pierce (the red-bordered set), brought only $25, probably because of the fact that it had a small chip under the rim. A chipped Lincoln dinner plate, however, brought $140, and a centennial reproduction of the Lincoln service, a dessert plate, brought $100. It also had a chip.

A Ulysses S. Grant plate, "Valanced and buff-bordered interrupted by the medallioned arms of the U.S.; the cavetto finely painted with a spray of pink and white morning glories," bore the legend on the reverse, "Administration U. S. Grant" and was also a centennial copy. It brought $75, as did the following plate, which was the same as the first except that the flower in the center was "a branch of flowering pink and cream variegated camellias with buds."

Prices at this auction for the Hayes plates were also somewhat disappointing. Two oyster plates were auctioned and brought only $50 apiece. A Chester Arthur Minton plate brought only $35; a Grover Cleveland porcelain saucer, "Starch blue border decorated in gold with floral motives, and inner radial border of buff and gold leafage; cavetto centring the initial 'C' " was said in the catalogue to have been from the collection of Mrs. Thomas J. Preston, Jr., Cleveland's widow. This plate, despite the authenticity, brought only $45.

Three more Harrison plates of dessert size, all from the collection of Mrs. Benjamin Harrison, according to the auction notes, brought $180, $70, and $70, respectively, although from the descriptions, they seem identical. Two Harrison tea plates brought the same price, $60, even though one was chipped. A plate attributed to William McKinley and described as having "a dark green border with four lancet motives enclosing pink poppy heads, flanked by gilded sprays of lilies," brought only $50.

The Wohl Washington Cincinnati plate showed up once more at an auction held by O. Rundle Gilbert in the Westchester County Center (New York) on September 13, 1960. This plate, formerly from the Wohl collection and recognizable in the photograph from a blemish in the porcelain, brought the staggering sum of $5,200. Mrs. Frances Clemson Cross had purchased the plate in the Wohl Parke-Bernet auction, and had she been alive to witness its sale in her own estate auction, she would have been gratified at the appreciation of her investment. (See Fig. 39.)

Another interesting item of the Cross estate auction was number 310, a "very rare James Madison plate" (again, really Buchanan). The note in this 1960 auction catalogue advises the auction goers that "up to 1949 only five pieces were known to be in existence that survived the burning of the White House by the British in 1814, then during the Truman Administration two more pieces were discovered in one of the upper closets." It seems ludicrous that White House historians, who should know better, would have released this story to the press. It is unlikely that these plates could have remained hidden in a closet in the White House, survived a burning, numerous renovations, and what one might hope were thorough house cleanings for over 150 years! In spite of this, the plate, in contrast with the other Presidential china offered for sale in this auction, sold for $550, twice as much as it had brought five years earlier at Parke-Bernet.

Several plates from the Hayes set were sold at the Cross auction, bringing prices ranging from $65 for the "wolf baying at the moon" plate that Mrs. Cross had probably purchased at the Wohl auction, to $90 for a ten-inch plate with "cream background with young chickens in strawberry bed."

A Grant plate with a green and gold border containing the American shield and *E Pluribus Unum* and with painted lavender and yellow flowers with green wavy leaves in the center brought $190; another Grant plate with a tulip in the center and having an orange and gold border sold for the same price, even though it bore the centennial reproduction mark "Administration U. S. Grant" on the reverse.

The latest publicized price for a piece of Presidential china should warm the hearts of all collectors. *New York Times* Antiques Editor Marvin Schwartz reported in that newspaper on February 22, 1969, that a George Washington Cincinnati plate, the same that had sold for $1,550 in 1954 and for $5,200 in 1960, was auctioned at the Astor Galleries in New York. Purchased by a dealer, it brought $7,000.

Author's Note

No one likes to be responsible for exploding legends, especially when they are bound up with our national heroes. The subject of the plates from which our heads of state have eaten is hardly one that will have any lasting effect on American history, no matter how often the attributions change as more information is gathered. However, the manner in which conclusions have been drawn concerning Presidential china is often applied to other areas of American history. Often scholarly interest comes too late, when much of the documentation has disappeared, and this leads to the perpetuation of legend rather than truth.

Personal feelings and political prejudice often have colored history, and we must learn to discount these, too, when studying our past. It is interesting that the work involved in protecting and procuring historical artifacts and works of art for the White House has only been continued from one administration to the next when the two administrations have been of the same political party. Mrs. John F. Kennedy seemed to understand this problem when she suggested that the collections at the White House be placed under a committee and that a curator be hired so that each First Lady would no longer have to feel responsible for their preservation.

Whether this system will work remains to be seen. With a change of administrations and a change of curators come press releases from the White House that can minimize the work of any previous First Lady in attempting to bring continuity to the historical objects, art, and decoration of the building. An example is an article published in the *New York Times* on Monday, July 27, 1970, which quotes Mr. Clement Conger, the present White House curator. Mr. Conger, who admits in this article that he is "not a professional curator, just an advanced amateur," said that Mrs. Aristotle Onassis (formerly Mrs. John F. Kennedy) "created an optical illusion that the White House contained a great collection of American antiques. Everyone has the mistaken impression that everything has been done. But nothing is further from the truth."

In this same article, Mr. Conger complained that "Mrs. Kennedy got a bit carried away with French decor and furnishings in [the Blue Room]." He said that the various renovations of the White House had "not been completely successful."

The truth is that it is seldom that one woman's taste in decorations for a house will completely satisfy another. In the same article, Mr. Conger said that Mrs. Nixon was not concerned about leaving her mark on the White House. "But it worries her terribly that the house doesn't look better." This pattern seems to have continued throughout the history of the White House. It has been just as true of the state china services of former administrations. Many of the patterns of White House china could easily have been reordered, but the desire of most First Ladies to choose their own plates has been one way for each to leave "her mark" on the home that she occupies for a brief period.

Criticism of the taste of a previous First Lady is usually the rule rather than the exception in the White House, and although the committee set up during the Kennedy and Johnson administrations must pass on all purchases or changes in the public rooms, the desires of the current First Lady are bound to be given careful consideration.

Interestingly, purchases for the White House public rooms, designated in Public Law 87-286 as "the principal corridor on the ground floor and the principal public rooms on the first floor" are paid for in part from the sale of THE WHITE HOUSE: AN HISTORIC GUIDE written by the first curator of the White House,

Mrs. John N. Pearce, who was hired during the Kennedy administration. Mrs. Pearce was followed by William V. Elder III, James R. Ketchum and Clement E. Conger, present curator. During the Kennedy administration Mrs. Mabel Walker, formerly housekeeper in the White House, completed the first comprehensive catalogue of all White House furnishings in various government storage areas. All objects were photographed at this time.

Neither the photographs nor the catalogue records are available for study by anyone outside of the White House. The guide book, which sells in enormous quantities to the thousands of citizens who tour the public rooms of the White House, was written under great pressure from Mrs. Kennedy who was anxious to raise money as quickly as possible to pay for purchases and improvements in the Executive Mansion.

Research in the decorative or fine arts cannot be rushed. It is unfortunate that even one erroneous attribution, that of calling the Buchanan centerpiece a "punchbowl" and "probably Jackson," appears in a book that is sold in quantity at the White House. Respect for truth and scholarship in the arts should begin at the top. It is obvious that a great deal more research is necessary in order to identify definitely many of the historical objects that represent our past Presidents and their families. The White House china collection, the only continuing collection representative of every family who lived in that historic building, would be an excellent place for that research to begin.

Bibliography

BOOKS

Baldridge, Letitia. *Of Diamonds and Diplomats.* Boston: Houghton Mifflin Company, 1968.

Buchanan, Wiley T., Jr., and Gordon, Arthur. *Red Carpet at the White House.* New York: E. P. Dutton & Co., Inc., 1964.

Butt, Archie. *The Letters of Archie Butt.* Garden City, N.Y.: Doubleday & Company, Inc., 1924.

Cable, Mary. *The Avenue of the Presidents.* Boston: Houghton Mifflin Company, 1969.

Camehl, Ada Walker. *The Blue-China Book.* New York: Tudor Publishing Co., 1948.

Cannon, Poppy, and Brooks, Patricia. *The Presidents' Cookbook.* New York: Funk & Wagnalls, Inc., 1968.

Colman, Edna M. *Seventy-five Years of White House Gossip.* Garden City, N.Y.: Doubleday & Company, Inc., 1926.

Crook, William H. *Memories of the White House.* Boston: Little, Brown and Company, 1911.

Cross, Wilbur, and Novotny, Ann. *White House Weddings.* New York: David McKay Co., Inc., 1967.

Daniels, Jonathan. *Washington Quadrille: The Dance Beside the Documents.* Garden City, N.Y.: Doubleday & Co., Inc., 1968.

Earle, Alice Morse. *China Collecting in America.* New York: Charles Scribner's Sons, 1892.

Furman, Bess. *White House Profile.* Indianapolis, Ind.: The Bobbs-Merrill Co., Inc., 1951.

Gibbs, Margaret. *The D.A.R.* New York: Holt, Rinehart & Winston, Inc., 1969.

Gray, Robert Keith. *Eighteen Acres Under Glass.* Garden City, N.Y.: Doubleday & Co., Inc., 1962.

Holloway, Laura C. *The Ladies in the White House, or in the Homes of the Presidents.* Philadelphia: Bradley & Company, 1880.

Hoover, Irwin Hood. *42 Years in the White House.* Boston: Houghton Mifflin Company, 1934.

Hurd, Charles. *The White House Story.* New York: Hawthorn Books, Inc., 1966.

Ingram, J. S. *The Centennial Exposition Described and Illustrated.* Philadelphia: Hubbard Brothers, 1877.

James, Marquis. *The Life of Andrew Jackson.* Indianapolis, Ind.: The Bobbs-Merrill Co., Inc., 1938.

Jeffries, Ona Griffin. *In and Out of the White House: From Washington to the Eisenhowers.* New York: Wilfrid Funk, 1960.

Jervis, W. P. *European China.* China Classics, vol. 3. Watkins Glen, N.Y.: Century House, Inc., 1953. Reprint of "Rough Notes on Pottery" printed in 1896.

Johnson, Lady Bird. *A White House Diary.* New York: Holt, Rinehart & Winston, Inc., 1970.

Karsner, David. *Andrew Jackson, The Gentle Savage.* New York: Brentano, 1929.

Kiplinger, W. M. *Washington is Like That.* New York: Harper & Brothers, Publishers, 1942.

Moore, N. Hudson. *The Old China Book.* New York: Frederick A. Stokes Company, 1903.

Parks, Lillian Rogers, and Leighton, Frances Spatz. *My Thirty Years Backstairs at the White House.* New York: Fleet Press Corporation, 1961.

Prindiville, Kathleen. *First Ladies*. New York: The Macmillan Company, 1932.

Spargo, John. *Early American Pottery and China*. Garden City, N.Y.: Garden City Publishing Co., Inc., 1926.

Steeholm, Clara, and Steeholm, Hardy. *The House at Hyde Park*. New York: The Viking Press, Inc., 1950.

Taft, Mrs. William Howard. *Recollections of Full Years*. New York: Dodd, Mead & Co., 1915.

Taylor, Mrs. Robert Coleman. *Liberty China and Queen's Ware*. Garden City, N.Y.: Doubleday & Co., Inc., 1924.

Truett, Randle Bond. *The White House*. New York: Hastings House, Publishers, Inc., 1949.

White House Historical Association. *The White House: An Historic Guide*. Washington, D.C., The White House Historical Association, 1964.

Willets, Gilson. *Inside History of the White House*. New York: The Christian Herald, Bible House, 1908.

Wolff, Perry. *A Tour of the White House With Mrs. John F. Kennedy*. Garden City, N.Y.: Doubleday & Company, Inc., 1962.

Wood, Serry. *Haviland-Limoges*. China Classics, vol. 2. Watkins Glen, N.Y.: Century House, Inc., 1951.

AUCTION CATALOGUES

Catalogue of the Governor Caleb Lyon Collection of Oriental and Occidental Ceramics—Belonging to Mrs. N. D. Lyon. April 24, 1876, Henry D. Minor, Auctioneer. New York.

Select Early American Furniture & Silver, American Presidential China, Oriental Lowestoft Porcelain 1770–1795, Staffordshire Lustre and Other Transfer-Printed Historical Ware, Historical Landscape Paintings, Early American Glass, Paperweights, Bibelots and other Decorative Objects from the Collection of Stanley S. Wohl, Annapolis, Md.; April 30 and May 1, 1954. Parke-Bernet Galleries, Inc. New York.

Fine Early American and English Furniture and Clocks, Silver, Paintings & Miniatures, Rare Oriental Lowestoft, Porcelain & Presidential China, Property of Dr. Hugh G. Hamilton, Kansas City, Mo., and from the Collections of Stanley S. Wohl, Annapolis, Md., Sol. M. Flock, Philadelphia, Pa. and from other owners. March 25 and 26, 1955. Parke-Bernet Galleries, Inc., New York.

The Collection of the Late Frances Clemson Cross, Chinese Export, 19th Century English & Continental Porcelains, Antique Oriental Rugs, Stevengraphs. Westchester County Center, September 13, 1960. O. Rundle Gilbert, Auctioneer.

MUSEUM CATALOGUES AND PUBLICATIONS

Dinner With the Presidents. Art Institute of Chicago. October 27 through December 3, 1961. Hans Huth, Curator of Decorative Arts.

Klapthor, Margaret Brown. *White House China of the Lincoln Administration in the Museum of History and Technology.* Washington, D.C.: Smithsonian Press, 1967.

The Mount Vernon Ladies Association. *The Mount Vernon China, An Illustrated Catalogue—with Historical Notes.* Mount Vernon, Va.: The Mount Vernon Ladies Association, 1949.

Terry, James. *A Descriptive Catalogue of a Portion of the Contents of my Colonial Dining Hall at my Home, No. 78 Wethersfield Avenue, Comprising Historical Furniture, Silver, Prints, Portraits and Historical China.* Waterbury, Conn.: Mattatuck Museum, 1905.

NEWSPAPER AND MAGAZINE ARTICLES

Aikman, Lonnelle. "Inside the White House." *National Geographic Magazine,* January 1961. pp. 1-43

Anderson, Mary F. "Dishes for the White House." *Americana,* April 1937, pp. 221-244

Baker, Abby Gunn. "The China of the Presidents." *Munsey's Magazine,* December 1903. pp. 321-329

———. "Historic China of the White House." *Arts and Decoration,* January 1922. pp. 195-197

———. "The White House Collection of Presidential Ware." *The Century Magazine,* October 1908. pp. 828-841

Davis, Theodore R. "Presidential Porcelain of a Century." *Ladies' Home Journal,* May 1899. p. 4

"For the President's Table." *Ladies' Home Journal,* June 1968. pp. 60-63

"F.Y.I., 'Presidential Dinnerware.'" *Home Furnishings Daily,* 28 May 1970, p. 2

"George Washington's China Sold." *China, Glass and Lamps,* 22 May 1895. p. 20

Herring, Lois, and Herring, Clint. "Haviland Reissues of Presidential China." *Spinning Wheel,* October 1970.

MacPherson, Myra. "New China Service for the White House is Pure Americana." *New York Times,* 10 May 1968. p. 4

Schwartz, Marvin D. "Antiques: First in Plates." *New York Times,* 22 February 1969. p. 22

Thomsen, J. K. "The White House China Room." *Antiques Journal,* July 1961. pp. 8-11

Robertson, Nan. "2 Long-Buried Bins Yield White House Artifacts." *New York Times,* 25 November 1969. p. 4

Waterhouse, Dorothy S. "Presidential China." *Antiques,* November 1948. pp. 330-332

"The White House Before the Kennedys and After—Now What?" *New York Times,* 27 July 1970. p. 30

"White House China." *China, Glass and Lamps,* 30 November 1892. p. 21

PROMOTIONAL PUBLICATIONS

First Lady's Choice: Dinnerware Selected by Presidents' Wives for the White House. From the Americana Collection of B. T. Babbitt, Inc.

State Dinner Service: Administration of President Ulysses S. Grant, 1869–1877. Klapthor, Margaret Brown. Haviland and Company, New York.

The White House Porcelain Service, 1879. Haviland Company, New York.

Index

Adams, Abigail (Mrs. John), 23; describes WH in 1800, 22; first First Lady to occupy WH, 21

Adams, John, 24, 103, 152, 155; favors European etiquette, 23; first President in WH, 21; holds first New Year's reception, 22

Adams, John Quincy, 40, 152, 154; entertains Lafayette at WH, 38; orders inventory of WH furnishings, 39; uses Monroe plate as state china, 39

Adams, Louisa Johnson (Mrs. John Quincy), furnishes East Room with French imports and draws ire of husband's enemies, 38-9

Alexis, Grand Duke of Russia, WH guest, 83

American Bicentennial, 146-8

Angoulême pottery, purchased by George Washington, described, 17

Antique Journal, 75

Arthur, Chester Alan, 8, 148, 159; "modernizes" WH, 93; orders auction of unwanted items, 92, 151; unconcerned about historical value, 92

Arthur, Prince, of England, WH guest, 78

Art Institute of Chicago, 23, 73

Astor Galleries, New York City, auctioneers, 160

auctions, of "Cincinnati" plate, reported February 22, 1969, 160; of Governor Lyon collection, April 24, 1876, 26, 151; of WH items, 1881, 92, 151; of Wohl collection, April 30-May 1, 1954, 157; of Wohl collection (second auction), March 26, 1955, 158

Baker, Mrs. Abby Gunn, 5, 7, 10, 64, 65; approached by General Bingham to save Presidential china, 4; becomes recognized expert on subject, 6; cites prices paid at auctions, 151; describes Hayes china, 87-8; invited by Mrs. McKinley to study china, 4; tells how damaged WH china was disposed of, 150-1; writes about Mrs. Benjamin Harrison and porcelain bowl restored, 63; writes press release describing Wilson china, with quotations from, 115-17

Bingham, General Theodore A., suggests care of WH furnishings to Mrs. Baker, 4
Bliss, Elizabeth Taylor, daughter of President Taylor, his official hostess, 52
Blue-China Book, The (Camehl), 65
Boteler, J. W. and Brother, 78
Buchanan, James, 57, 67, 69, 154, 157, 160; only bachelor President, 58; probably purchased WH china with own money, 62; WH social life improves during term, 58
Bureau of Public Buildings and Grounds, WH china collection placed under supervision of, 6
Burtis, Miss Cornelia, 55
Butt, Archie, WH historian, describes Mrs. Theodore Roosevelt and china, 106-108; writes about Mrs. Taft's parties, 109
Butt, Mrs. Lewis F., 106

Camehl, Ada Walker, 65; describes Madison china, 66
Canton china, favored in U.S., 67; gift to Martha Washington, 16; porcelain at Mount Vernon, 13; Taylor soup plate in WH collection, 53
Castleton china, Eisenhower service plates, described, 134; L. B. Johnson service, described, 140-1
Caughley pottery, service owned by George Washington, 17
Century Magazine, The, 64
Chiang Kai-shek, Madame, WH guest, 127
Chicago World's Fair, 1893, 97; *see also* exhibitions
china: ceramic art in America, 44; first use of red, white, and blue shield, 51; French dinner service for Jackson, described, 40; porcelain punch bowl for Jackson, described, 41-2; state china for Polk, described, 51; *see also* under Dresden, Minton, etc.
China Collecting in America (Earle), 4, 26, 63
China Collection, Presidential; *see* White House: China Collection
China, Glass and Lamps, 156
China Room; *see* White House: China Room
Churchill, Winston, WH guest, 127
"Cincinnati" china, 156, 158, 159, 160; bought by Washington, described, examples in Mount Vernon, WH collection, Smithsonian Institution, Metropolitan Museum of Art, 14
Cleveland, Frances Folsom (Mrs. Grover), children, 97; husband's illness, 97; predicts husband's re-election, 96-7; WH guest, 112; WH wedding, 95-6

Cleveland, Grover, 5, 151, 159; bachelor at election, sister acts as hostess until his marriage, two nonconsecutive terms, 95

Cleveland, Rose, WH hostess for brother, 95

Conger, Clement E., Curator of WH, 9, 162, 163

Congress, appropriate funds for furnishing or renovating WH, 31, 43, 58, 70, 74, 105; attacks Van Buren for buying French china, 44; Monroe warns concerning WH relics, 10, 31, 37; passes measure requiring all WH furnishings to be of domestic origin, 40

Constantine, Grand Duke of Russia, WH guest, 83

Coolidge, Calvin, 104; entertains many famous WH guests, 122

Coolidge, Grace Goodhue (Mrs. Calvin), popular and gracious hostess, 122; portrait of her with dog, only painting in WH China Room, 3, 123

Coolidge, John, son of President Coolidge, donates family plates to WH collection, described, 123

Cooper, James Fenimore, describes dinner at WH with James Monroe, 33-4

Copeland/Spode plates belonging to Coolidge, described, 123

Copenhagen china pattern in Hoover display in WH collection, 126

Cox, Edward Finch, marries Tricia Nixon in WH Rose Garden, 143

Crook, Colonel William, WH employee, 64, 96; buys Lincoln pitcher for $2.50, 151

Cross, Mrs. Frances Clemson, 159, 160

Crump, William, of WH staff, purchases china at auction, 151

Crystal Palace Exhibition of 1853; *see* exhibitions

Crystal Palace Exhibition Publication, describes china design offered to President Pierce, 67

Custine, Comte de, owner of Niderviller factory, presents table service to George Washington, 17

Custis family, gives souvenir china to Lafayette, 16

Custis, George Washington Parke, beneficiary of Martha Washington, 14, 16

Custis, Martha Dandridge; *see* Washington, Martha Dandridge (Mrs. George)

Custis, Nellie; *see* Lewis, Nellie Custis (Mrs. Lawrence)

Dagoty dessert service ordered by James Monroe, described, 36; considered state china, 37

Davis, Theodore, 8, 67, 87, 89, 136, 158; describes Jackson china, 63-4; designs Hayes state china, 84

Descriptive Catalogue of a Portion of the Contents of my Colonial Dining Hall at my Home, No. 78 Wethersfield Avenue, Comprising Historical Furniture, Silver, Prints, Portraits and Historical China, A (Terry), 17

Designs by an American Artist Illustrating Exclusively American Fauna and Flora, subtitle of Haviland publication of WH porcelain, 84

"Dinner with the Presidents," exhibit at Chicago, 1961, 23, 73

Dole, Sanford B., WH guest, 102
Donelson, Mrs. Emily, WH hostess for Jackson, 41
Dresden compote from Polk family, described, 51; favored by McKinleys, 103
Duncanson Brothers, Auctioneers, Washington, D.C., 92, 151

Earle, Mrs. Alice Morse, 5, 26, 29, 63
Eastin, Mary Ann, bride in WH, 42
Edinburgh, Duke of, WH guest, 132
Edward VII (as Prince of Wales), WH guest, 60, 69
Edward VIII (as Prince of Wales), WH guest, 122
Eisenhower, David, 135
Eisenhower, Dwight David, 7, 8, 133
Eisenhower, Julie Nixon (Mrs. David), 143
Eisenhower, Mamie Doud (Mrs. Dwight D.), 121, 123; adds china of five Presidents not previously represented, 8, 134; has WH collection rearranged chronologically, 134; orders only service plates, described, 135; personal dinner set, described, 135; strong sense of history, 9; places WH collection under custody of Smithsonian Institution, 10; uses imagination and humor in entertaining, 136
Elder, William V., III, second curator of WH, 163
Elizabeth, Princess, of England, guest at Blair House, 132
Elizabeth, Queen of England, WH guest, 128
Etruria, England, 106, 118
exhibitions, Crystal Palace, 1853, 69, 70; displays china designed for President of U.S., 57; design described in publication of, 67; "Dinner with the Presidents," 1961, Chicago, 23, 73; New York World's Fair, 1939, 130

Farrar, Richard, and Company of London, 13
Fillmore, Abigail Powers (Mrs. Millard), begins WH library, 54; continues subdued social life of predecessor despite poor health, 55; dies one month after leaving Washington, 55
Fillmore, Mary Abigail, assistant WH hostess with her mother, 54-5
Fillmore, Millard, 54-5
Folsom, Frances; *see* Cleveland, Frances Folsom (Mrs. Grover)
French porcelain, becomes fashionable after Revolutionary War, 14; from Governor Lynn collection sold at auction, 152-4
Furman, Bess, 104

Gardiner, Julia; *see* Tyler, Julia Gardiner (Mrs. John)
Garfield, James Abram, 90; family plate, described, 91; reproductions of plate, 148
Garfield, Lucretia Rudolph (Mrs. James A.), begins research on WH historic objects, 90
George II, King of Greece, WH guest, 127

George VI, King of England, at New York World's Fair, 1939, 130; WH guest, 127
Gilbert, O. Rundle (auctioneer), Westchester County, N.Y., 159
Governor Caleb Lyon Collections of Oriental and Occidental Ceramics (catalogue), 151-2; Jefferson export china, described, 26
Grant, Julia Dent (Mrs. Ulysses S.), as WH hostess, 81; expands WH social life, 76-7
Grant, Nellie, 76; WH wedding to Algernon Sartoris, described, 80
Grant, Ulysses Simpson, 152, 157, 158; plate in Wohl collection, described, 159; reproductions of plate, 146-8; WH social life, 76-7; memoirs, 81

Halsted, Anna Roosevelt (Mrs. James A.), donates Roosevelt china to WH collection, described, 128-9
Harding, Florence Kling (Mrs. Warren G.), beset by poor health and unhappy marriage, 120; has WH silverware goldplated to match Monroe *surtout*, 120; takes little interest in duties as WH hostess, 120
Harding Home and Museum, 134; sends representative china to WH collection, 121
Harding, Warren Gamaliel, 134; entertains lavishly, 120
Harper's Weekly, 84
Harrison, Anna Symes (Mrs. William Henry), attitude toward public life, 46
Harrison, Benjamin, 5, 98, 140, 158, 159
Harrison, Caroline Scott (Mrs. Benjamin), 62-4; agitates for new WH, 98-100; designs own state china but dies before using, 101; first president general of DAR, 99; fond of orchids, 99; lavish, though infrequent WH entertainment, 99; paints *A White House Orchid*, 136; remodels WH facilities by stretching Congressional funds, 99; saves and restores WH china, 4, 100; teaches ceramic painting, 99
Harrison, William Henry, 46-7
Haughwout, E. V., and Company, 69, 70, 75
Haviland and Company, 57, 78; publishes book on WH porcelain, with complete story of Hayes china, 84-7
Haviland-Limoges, 67, 148, 149, 158; centennial reproductions of WH china, 144; commemorative plates for American Bicentennial, 147-8; china for Buchanan, 72; for Garfield, 91; for Grant, 84; for Benjamin Harrison, 101; for Hayes, 84-9; for Mary Lincoln, 73; for McKinley, 103; patterns in WH, 157; for Pierce, 57; Franklin D. Roosevelt presentation plate, 129; turkey platter from Hayes service added to WH collection, 136
Haviland, Theodore, 129-30
Haviland, Theodore, II, 148
Hayes, Eliza Monroe, daughter of President Monroe, often substitutes for mother at WH functions, 34
Hayes, Lucy Webb (Mrs. Rutherford B.), education and social graces, 82-3; plans WH china collection and moves it incomplete to Ohio, 4; state china, described, 84; duplicated for sale to public, 7; WH social life, 83

Hayes, Rutherford Birchard, 5, 8, 63, 82, 90, 157, 159; dinner plate, described, 158; reproductions of, 148; state china, described, 84; 25th wedding anniversary at WH, 83-4

Hermitage, The, home of Andrew Jackson, 41

Holloway, Laura C., comments on Mrs. John Quincy Adams' health, 39; on Mrs. William Henry Harrison, 46; on Harriet Lane, President Buchanan's hostess, 59; on Nellie Grant's wedding, 80-1; on Mrs. Franklin Pierce, 56

Hoover, Herbert Clark, 134; entertains elegantly with many guests, 124-5; Wedgwood dinner service in WH collection, described, 126

Hoover, I. W., 97, 110

Hoover, Lou Henry (Mrs. Herbert C.), comments by WH maid concerning, 125; entertains elegantly, 124-5; restores Monroe Room, 124

Houckgeest, Andrea van Braam, gives Cantonese service to Martha Washington, 16

Hyde Park, home of Franklin D. Roosevelt, 127-9

Imari (Japanese), pattern chosen by President Arthur, 94

Jackson, Andrew, 29, 38, 44, 66-7, 154; china, described, 63-4; final reception damages WH furnishings, 43; inaugural reception breaks Monroe china and glassware, 40

Jackson, Rachel Donelson (Mrs. Andrew), 64; attitude toward Presidency and WH, 41; dies before husband's inauguration, 41

Jackson, Sarah Yorke (Mrs. Andrew, Jr.), mother of baby born in WH, 41; second hostess for Jackson, 41

Jaffray, Mrs. Elizabeth, first housekeeper of WH, 110

Jefferson, Thomas, 140, 152, 154, 155; comments concerning, by John Adams, 23; east and west wings originally planned by, restored to WH, 105; furnishes at least 20 rooms of WH, 27; known for good taste and hospitality, most famous meal given while Secretary of State, 24; shakes hands with guests, 25; suffers financial losses, household effects sold at auction after death of, 26

Johnson, Andrew, 73, 74, 134, 148; state of WH after Civil War, 74

Johnson, Claudia "Lady Bird" Taylor (Mrs. Lyndon B.), entertains frequently and with originality, 139-40; her book most complete record of an administration by a First Lady, 139; meets with Tiffany designers to choose china, described, 140; strong sense of history, 9; uses Hayes china, 89

Johnson, Eliza McCardle (Mrs. Andrew), her state of health, 74

Johnson, Lyndon Baines, 139

Kennedy, Jacqueline Bouvier (Mrs. John F.), conscientious WH hostess, 137; innovations in WH dinner parties, uses historic china, 138; obtains pieces of Monroe china for WH collection and Smithsonian Institution, 37, 138; sparks passage of law prohibiting future sale or disposal of WH items, 6, 137; strong sense of history, 9; suggests WH collection be placed under curator, 161

Kennedy, John Fitzgerald, entertains in elegant, relaxed atmosphere, with superb entertainment, 137; no effort made to catalogue china collection since term of, 8

Kerr, J. K., of Philadelphia, 73

Ketchum, James R., third curator of WH, 58, 163

Ladies' Home Journal, 63, 158

Ladies of the White House, The, or, In the Home of the Presidents (Holloway), 39

Lafayette, Marquis de, given souvenir china by Custis family, 16; WH guest, 38

Lane, Harriet, 60, 69; niece and ward of President Buchanan, his official WH hostess, 59

Lee, Colonel Henry, purchases "Cincinnati" table service on order of George Washington, price paid, 14

Lee House, 132

Lee, William, 65

Lenox, china for Wilson, described, 113-7, china for Harding, described, 121; for F. D. Roosevelt as state china, described, 128; dinner service for Truman, described, 132; service plates from F. D. Roosevelt term in WH storage, described, 129

Lenox Pottery, Trenton, New Jersey, history of, 113; made first American state china, 115

Lenox, Walter Scott, founder of Lenox Pottery, 115

Lewis, Mary Ann, bride in WH, 42

Lewis, Major William Berkely, member of Jackson's "Kitchen Cabinet," 42

Lewis, Mrs. H. L. Daingerfield, preserved blue pottery vessel belonging to Nellie Custis Lewis, 20

Lewis, Nellie Custis (Mrs. Lawrence), 20

"Liberty China," described, 118; manufacture and distribution, 118; proposed and designed by Mrs. R. C. Taylor, 117-8; used at WH, 119

Library of Congress, asked by Mrs. Garfield to help trace history of WH and contents, 90

Limoges (China); *see* Haviland-Limoges

Limoges, France, 67, 69, 73, 78

Lincoln, Abraham, 5, 6, 63, 70, 152, 158; reproductions of plate, 146, 148

Lincoln, Mary Todd (Mrs. Abraham), 57, 69, 74, 158; buys duplicate set of WH china with her own initials, 72-3; other china, described, 70-2; shopping habits, 70

Lindbergh, Charles A., WH guest, 122

Longworth, Nicholas, marries Alice Roosevelt at WH, 104-5

Lowestoft, "Cincinnati" china sold at auction, 157

Lyon, Governor Caleb, collection sold at auction, 151; Presidential china in, described, 152-6

Lyon, Mrs. H. D., 151

Madison, Dorothea "Dolley" Payne (Mrs. James), 44, 66, 157; describes burning of WH, 28-9; French china reputedly hers, described, 30; hostess for Jefferson, 27; lives in Octagon House after WH burned, 29; "most popular woman in U.S.," 33

Madison, James, 66, 67, 152, 154, 160; china destroyed by British, 65; dinner plate in second Wohl auction, 158; entertains lavishly, 27

Marie, Queen of Romania, WH guest, 122

"Martha Washington" plate, one of three names most associated with Washingtons, 14; centennial reproduction, 148; described, 16, 144; most often reproduced, 144

Meissen, favored by McKinleys, 103; plate in WH collection from John Quincy Adams, 39; "Onion" pattern, chosen by President Arthur, 94; plate from John Quincy Adams in Smithsonian Institution, 39

mementos of visit, guests presented with china, 14

Metropolitan Museum of Art, 145; "Cincinnati" table service at, 14

Miner, Henry D. (auction gallery), New York City, 151

Minton china, 68; dessert service in Taft display in WH collection, 112; Eisenhower family china, 135; plate belonging to President Arthur, 159

"Monogram," one of three names of tea service most associated with Washington, 14; centennial reproduction, 148; described, 16, 144

Monroe, Elizabeth Kortwright (Mrs. James), 35; criticized by Washington society, 34; European ideas antagonize society, 33; good taste unquestioned, 37

Monroe, James, 31, 60, 140, 152, 158; accustomed to "best" all his life, 35; asks Congress for governmental supervision of WH and furnishings, 31; china and glassware destroyed by boisterous Jackson reception, 40; early warnings to Congress ignored, 37; French purchases not criticized, 39; personal china and furniture purchased by government for WH, 32; realized problems of care and preservation with changes of administration, 10; strong sense of history, 31; two patterns of china, described, 36; *surtout de table*, centerpiece from France, described, 33; repaired after damage, 44; WH silver gold-plated to match, 120

Monticello, home of Thomas Jefferson, 24-5

Moravian Institute, Salem, North Carolina, 50

Morris, Gouverneur, commissioned by Washington to purchase table ornaments in Paris, 14

Morris, William, 93

Mount Vernon, home of George Washington, 28; "Cincinnati" table service at, 14; proper study of china and relics, 10; Washington's china loaned by Harvard, 17; Washington returns to, after Presidency, 14

Moustier, Comte de, French minister to U.S., 14

Munsey's Magazine, 63, 87, 150

Museum of Fine Arts, Boston, owns Sèvres plate belonging to John Adams, 23

McCaffree, Mrs., secretary to Mrs. Eisenhower, 134

McKinley, Ida Saxton (Mrs. William), 158; arranges centennial of WH, 103; health prevents her being active WH hostess, 102; interest in WH china collection not realized, 5; invites Mrs. Baker to study Presidential china, 4; own china and tea service, described, 103

McKinley, William, 3, 5, 159; concern about wife's health, 102; family china in WH collection, 8

Nast pottery, French porcelain purchased by George Washington, 17

National Archives, 5, 10; vouchers for French china purchased by Monroe, described, 35-6

Nesbitt, Mrs. Henrietta, WH housekeeper for F. D. Roosevelt, 127; describes china used, 128; English monarchs' visit, 128; pilferage by WH souvenir hunters, 130

New York Exhibition Illustrated, 69

New York Times, The, 160, 162

New York World's Fair, 1939, 130; *see also* exhibitions

Niderviller table service presented to George Washington, described, 17

Nixon, Patricia Ryan (Mrs. Richard M.), no plans yet to order new china, 143; using Truman china in one photograph, 143; worries about condition of WH, 162

Nixon, Richard Milhous, 143, 148

Nixon, Tricia, marries Edward Finch Cox in WH Rose Garden, 143

Oak View, residence purchased and used by Clevelands during Presidency, 96

Octagon House, used by Madison after WH burned, 29

Old House, The, home of Adams family in Quincy, Mass., 23

Onassis, Mrs. Aristotle, 162; *see also* Kennedy, Jacqueline (Mrs. John F.)

Pageot, Alphonse, bridegroom in White House, 42

"Parian" ware, described, 67

Parke-Bernet Galleries, New York City, 65, 157-60

Parks, Lillian Rogers, White House maid, comments on Mrs. Hoover, 125

Patterson Mansion, occupied by Coolidges during WH repairs, 122

Patterson, Martha Johnson, daughter of President Andrew Johnson, assumes role of WH hostess, 74; redecorates judiciously and carefully, 74; elegant social life, described, 75

Pearce, Mrs. John N., first curator of WH, 162

"Pelican" centerpieces, purchased by Mrs. Lincoln, described, 71

Peter, King of Yugoslavia, WH guest, 127

Philadelphia, Pennsylvania, second capital of U.S., 13

Pierce, Franklin, 69, 152, 154, 158-9; installs furnace and other improvements in WH, 58; plate reproductions, 148; purchases china, described, 58; tragedies in personal life, 56

Pierce, Jane Appleton (Mrs. Franklin), 69; fragile health, 56; social life at WH, 56-7; tragedies in family, 56-7

Piette, Andre, 140

Plummer, William H. and Sons, New York City, 118

Polk, James Knox, 50, 154, 157; china first to use red, white, and blue shield, 51; Dresden compote and matching pieces state china, described, 51; frugality with regard to money, 51

Polk, Lucius Junius, bridegroom in WH, 42

Polk, Sarah Childress (Mrs. James K.), brings in own plate, 50; cleans out broken furnishings and china from WH, 50; her tastes subdued and devout, no gay parties or cardplaying, 50

Poplar Forest, lodge built as retreat by Jefferson, 25

Presidential china; auctions of, from private collections, 150; beginning of sorting and identification, 11; discussed by Mrs. Earle, 5; former disposal methods, 150-1; government records concerning, unavailable for study, 9; historical importance of, 4; legends surrounding make identification of plates almost impossible, 9-10; no photographs of reverse sides, 8; ordered by Grant, described, 78; plates purchased by dozen as needed, 5; purchased by Van Buren, criticized and described, 44; purchased on open market and not specially decorated or monogrammed, 6; vouchers for china purchases in National Archives, 5; press releases concerning, 7, 8, 115, 117; records of china purchased before 1817 not available for study, 9; reproductions, 144; *see also* White House: China Collection

Presidential Seal, standardized, 132

"President Wilson" design, first American china at WH, ordered by Woodrow Wilson, described, 115-17

Preston, Mrs. Thomas J., Jr., 159; *see also* Cleveland, Francis Folsom (Mrs. Grover)

Preston, Professor Thomas J., Jr., engaged to Frances Folsom Cleveland, 112

Public Law 87-286, designates WH public rooms, 162

Recollections of Full Years (Taft), 111

Revolutionary War, disrupted business with Staffordshire potters, 14

Rockingham ware, dish belonging to Jefferson in WH collection, 26

Roosevelt, Alice, marries Nicholas Longworth at WH, 104-5

Roosevelt, Anna Eleanor Roosevelt (Mrs. Franklin D.), modernized WH kitchen, more interested in renovation than redecoration, 130

Roosevelt, Edith Carow (Mrs. Theodore, 62, 104; becomes interested in Presidential china but refuses to purchase because donations should be from "patriotic" motives, 5; dedicated to finding authentic pieces, 6; places original cabinets for china in WH China Room, 7

Roosevelt, Franklin Delano, 7, 124, 140; entertains many important visitors, 127; large family very active, 127

Roosevelt, Theodore, Congress appropriates funds to renovate WH, 105; daughter's wedding, 104-5; orders Wedgwood for state service when no American pottery found suitable, 105; rebuilds WH west wing, 105

Rosenthal china, Eisenhower personal dinner set, described, 135

Royal Worcester, services used by Lincoln, described, 73

Sartoris, Algernon Charles Frederick, marries Nellie Grant at WH, 80

Select Early American Furniture and Silver, American Historical China, Paintings, Glass & Other Property from the Collection of Stanley S. Wohl, Annapolis, Md. and from other owners, (catalogue), 157

Sèvres china, used by Lincoln, 75; "Pelican" centerpieces purchased by Mrs. Lincoln, described, 71; plate from John Adams in Museum of Fine Arts, Boston, 23; state service for George Washington, described, 17; porcelain plate of George Washington in Governor Lyon collection, 156; vases purchased by Monroe still in use in WH, 33

Shaw, Major Samuel, first secretary, Order of the Cincinnati, 14, 157

Shenango China Company, porcelain plate made for Washington Bicentennial, 145-6

Singleton, Angelica, marries Van Buren's son, becomes official WH hostess, 44

Smithsonian Institution, 8, 26, 29, 138, 148; china collection, dispelling myths, surrounding, 11; "Cincinnati" table service at, 14; collection of Presidential china treated more as curiosity, 9; displayed in various period rooms, 10; given custody of Presidential china, 10; information on Lincoln china, 73; owns dish said to belong to Dolley Madison, described, 30, owns Meissen Onion plate from John Quincy Adams, 39

Society of the Cincinnati, table service bought by George Washington, 14

Soldier's Home, summer WH of Lincolns, 73

Spode, plates represent Coolidge in WH collection, 134

Staffordshire, blue willow pattern from Chinese, most popular in America, used by Presidential household in Philadelphia, 13; earthenware of Fillmore in WH collection, 55; ironstone belonging to Taft in WH collection, 112; plate belonging to Andrew Johnson, 75; platter belonging to Taylor in WH collection, 53; Pottery severely hurt by Revolutionary War, 14; ware sent to George Washington at Mount Vernon, 12

Stanton, Edwin M., Secretary of War under Lincoln, china belonging to, described, 79

"States," one of three names of tea service most associated with Washington, 14; centennial reproductions, 148; described, 16

Stuart, Gilbert, 65

Symons, Colonel Thomas W., superintendent of public buildings and grounds, interests Mrs. Theodore Roosevelt in china collection, 5

table setting, for dinner honoring Imperial Russian Grand Dukes, described, 83

Taft, Helen Herron (Mrs. William Howard), celebrates 25th wedding anniversary, 110-11; describes WH years in memoirs, 111; energetic WH hostess, 109; forced by illness to curtail activities, 110; gives engagement dinner for Mrs. Cleveland, 112; hires first WH housekeeper, 110; plans Potomac Park as promenade with cherry trees, 110; remembers using Monroe *surtout de table*, 112; strong force in husband's career, 109

Taft, William Howard, 134; hearty eater, 110; silver wedding anniversary party, 110-11; uses parties for politicking, 109

Taylor, Margaret Smith (Mrs. Zachary), attitude toward official life, 52-3

Taylor, Mrs. Robert Coleman, and "Liberty China" to raise money for "war sufferers"; makes stipulations about manufacture and sale; has plates for design destroyed at end of World War I, 117-18

Taylor, Zachary, 52-4, 152

Terry, James, catalogues large pottery vessel belong to Nellie Custis, 20; records historical china and furnishings, with documented Washington china, 17

Thomson, J. K., describes Lincoln china, 75

Tiffany and Company, New York City, 140; designers meet with Mrs. Lyndon Johnson, 139-40

Tiffany, Louis Comfort, hired by President Arthur to redecorate WH, 93

Tresseman and Vogt, made Benjamin Harrison china, 101

Truman, Bess Wallace (Mrs. Harry S), image as American housewife, well liked by public, 131

Truman, Harry S, 7, 131, 150; air conditioning for WH, 132; convinces Congress to rebuild WH and moves to Blair House, 132; Lenox china, described, 132; standardizes Presidential Seal, 132; "Truman balcony," 132

Tyler, John, first Vice President to succeed to Presidency, 48

Tyler, Julia Gardiner (Mrs. John), marries President while still in office, has short but regal period as WH hostess, 49

Tyler, Letitia Christian (Mrs. John), year in WH described by son, 48-9

Tyler, Major Robert, describes social life in WH during father's term, 48-9

Union Fédérale des Mutils Combattants du Limousin presents Limoges service to F. D. Roosevelt, 129

United States, two hundredth anniversary, 10; 146-8

Van Buren, Hannah Hoes (Mrs. Martin), dies 17 years before husband's inauguration, 43

Van Buren, Major, oldest son and secretary of President, marries Angelica Singleton, 44

Van Buren, Martin, 152; china criticized and described, 44; Congress appropriates funds, then criticizes his efforts to refurbish WH, 45; personal tastes and habits, 43

Victoria, Queen, 58, 78; thanks President Buchanan for hospitality to Prince of Wales, 60

Walker, Mrs. Mabel, WH housekeeper, made first comprehensive catalogue of furnishings, 163

Washington, D.C., location discussed at Jefferson's most famous dinner, 24

Washington, George, 3, 152; at Jefferson's most famous dinner, 23; china in Governor Lyon collection, 156; "Cincinnati" china sold at auction, 157; given Niderviller table service, described, and purchases other French porcelain, 17; marriage, 12; moves to house formerly owned by French minister, purchases furnishings and French porcelain, 14

Washington, Martha Dandridge (Mrs. George), china in Governor Lyon collection, 156; given Cantonese service, bequeaths remainder to grandson, 16; marriage, 12; three patterns most closely associated with, 14; wills remainder of "Cincinnati" table service to grandson, 14

Wedgwood, china ordered by Cleveland, described, 96, and by Theodore Roosevelt, 104, 106; Colonnade pattern for T. Roosevelt, 148; creamware in Taft display in WH collection, 112; new plates for English monarchs' visit, 128; Queen's ware used by Kennedy in Georgetown home, 138; service donated by Hoover to WH collection, described, 125-6

Wedgwood, Josiah, 12, 106, 118

White House Diary, A (Johnson), 89, 139

White House, The (publication), 62

White House: An Historic Guide, The (Pearce), 162-3

White House China of the Lincoln Administration (Smithsonian Institution), 73

White House Historical Association, 62

White House Orchid, A, painting by Mrs. Benjamin Harrison, 136

White House Porcelain Service, The (Haviland), 84

White House Profile (Furman), 104

White House, broken furnishings cleared away by Mrs. Polk, 50; burned by British, 28; conditions when Fillmore took office, 54; furnishings first catalogued and photographed, 163; library begun by Mrs. Fillmore, 54; "modernized" under President Arthur, 93-4; not yet restored in 1817 after burning, 31; police guards first used to protect First Family, 50; preservation of relics stimulated by collection of Presidential china, and rules established to prevent removal of historic objects from WH, 6; prestige of social life, 35; public rooms designated by law, 162; received fresh food from Monticello farm, 24; renovated, 78; rebuilt, 132; condition during Cleveland's early administration, 96; weddings, described, 42

White House

Blue Room, 162; reception July 4, 1801, first of Independence Day tradition, 24; scene of Folsom-Cleveland wedding, 97

China Collection, 3, 148; Arthur china, described, 93-4; "Cincinnati" table service, 14; collected and restored by Mrs. Benjamin Harrison, 100; earliest published indication of interest in, 4; errors in guide book, 163; Fillmore Staffordshire earthenware, 55; first collection, 4; Garfield family plates, described, 91; General Bingham's interest in, 4; interest shown by Mrs. Benjamin Harrison, 4; Jefferson dish of Rockingham ware, 26; J. Q. Adams Meissen plate, 39; Lenox china from Harding Home and Museum, 121; Monroe dessert service obtained by Mrs. Kennedy, 138; Monroe plate in, 36; Mrs. Hayes removes incomplete collection to Ohio, 4; Mrs. Lyndon Johnson studies representative china before ordering service, 14; porcelain bowl centerpiece, described, 62, and alleged owners of, 62-69; should be open to public, 149; Taft Wedgwood plate, Staffordshire ironstone, and Minton dessert service in, 112; Taylor Staffordshire platter and other pieces in, 53; Taylor dinner plate, described, 49; W. H. Harrison pitcher, described, 47

China Room, 3; designed by Mrs. Wilson, 7; new cabinets and renovation, 8; open only to important guests, 9; painting by Mrs. Benjamin Harrison, donated, 136; portrait of Mrs. Coolidge, 123; should be open to general public, 11; used as breakfast room by Hoovers, 125

Diplomatic Reception Room, 3

East Room, 3; furnished by Mrs. John Quincy Adams, 38-9; reception and viewing of new Lyndon Johnson dinner service, 142; refurnished during Jackson's administration, 41; scene of WH wedding, 42; Grant-Sartoris wedding, 80

Green Room, Mrs. Lyndon Johnson receives Senate Ladies before lunch, 141

Monroe Room, restored by Mrs. Hoover, 124

Oval Room, scene of first New Year's reception, 1801, 22

Rose Garden, scene of Nixon-Cox wedding, 143

State Dining Room, Hallowe'en party in, 136; lunch for Senate Ladies by Mrs. Lyndon Johnson, 141; reopened by Martha Johnson Patterson, 75; scene of elaborate banquets under Grant, 76-77; used by Hoovers even when alone, 124

Wilhelmina, Queen of the Netherlands, WH guest, 127

Willow pattern, copies from Chinese by Staffordshire potters, becomes most popular American tableware, 1800-1850, 13; large quantities purchased by Washington for Presidential household in Philadelphia, 13

Wilson, Edith Bolling (Mrs. Woodrow), 128

Wilson, Woodrow, 7, 140; first president to purchase American china for state service, 113, 128; china described, 115; named for him, 117; second set, of Wedgwood, ordered, 117

Winterthur Museum, lends Monroe plate to WH collection, 37

Wohl auctions, first, 157; second, 158

Wohl collection, described, 157-9

Wohl, Stanley S., 157, 158

Worcester, John Adams teapot, described, 23

World, The (New York Newspaper), 72-3

"World's Fair plates," 129-30